Meredith Levy

Interactive

Workbook 3 with Downloadable Audio

CAMBRIDGE
UNIVERSITY PRESS

CAMBRIDGE
UNIVERSITY PRESS

University Printing House, Cambridge CB2 8BS, United Kingdom

One Liberty Plaza, 20th Floor, New York, NY 10006, USA

477 Williamstown Road, Port Melbourne, VIC 3207, Australia

314–321, 3rd Floor, Plot 3, Splendor Forum, Jasola District Centre,
New Delhi – 110025, India

79 Anson Road, #06–04/06, Singapore 079906

Cambridge University Press is part of the University of Cambridge.

It furthers the University's mission by disseminating knowledge in the pursuit of
education, learning and research at the highest international levels of excellence.

www.cambridge.org
Information on this title: www.cambridge.org/9780521712200

© Cambridge University Press 2012

First published 2012

20 19 18 17

Printed in Great Britain by CPI Group (UK) Ltd, Croydon CR0 4YY

A catalogue record for this publication is available from the British Library

ISBN 978-0-521-71220-0 Workbook with Downloadable Audio
ISBN 978-0-521-71219-4 Student's Book
ISBN 978-0-521-71221-7 Teacher's Book
ISBN 978-0-521-71222-4 Teacher's Resource Pack
ISBN 978-0-521-71223-1 Class Audio CDs
ISBN 978-0-521-14726-2 DVD (PAL)
ISBN 978-0-521-14727-9 DVD (NTSC)
ISBN 978-0-521-27961-1 Classware DVD-ROM
ISBN 978-0-521-27963-5 Testmaker CD-ROM and Audio CD

Contents

1	Get up and go!	4
2	Waste not, want not	10
3	Forces of nature	16
4	Friends 4ever	22
5	Top of the class	28
6	Who's got talent?	34
7	That's incredible!	40
8	Gaming and gadgets	46
9	Seeing is believing	52
10	Beyond words	58
11	Is it a crime?	64
12	Moving on	70

Grammar reference and Grammar practice	76
Irregular verbs	102
Phonemic chart	103

1 Get up and go!

1 Vocabulary

Fitness

a Choose the correct answer: A, B or C.

1 I keep .... by walking everywhere.

   A fitness   **B** active   **C** train

2 The runners are warming .... on the track before the race.

   A up   **B** down   **C** out

3 When you touch your toes, you .... your back, legs and arms.

   A stretch   **B** train   **C** fit

4 An acrobat's body is very strong and ....

   A energy   **B** flexible   **C** stretching

5 I'm going to work .... at the gym for an hour.

   A in   **B** out   **C** over

6 The athletics team .... on Wednesdays at the sports ground.

   A trains   **B** trainer   **C** training

7 Mountain biking is a very .... form of exercise.

   A flexible   **B** energetic   **C** strong

8 Doing sport helps to keep people .... and healthy.

   A fit   **B** fitting   **C** fitness

b Complete the sentences. Use words from Exercise 1a in the correct form.

This dancer is ^{1}s............................ as part of his exercise routine before he goes on stage. This is a good way to ^{2}w............................ before a performance.

If you aren't feeling very ^{3}e............................ and you often feel tired, it's probably because you aren't getting enough exercise or you're eating the wrong types of food.

Professional football players have to be very ^{4}f............................ . They ^{5}t............................ every week with their team at the football ground and they also ^{6}w............................ in the gym.

This woman is in her 60s but she is still very ^{7}a............................ . The exercise she is doing here keeps her back ^{8}f............................ so she can move and bend easily.

c Look at your answers for Exercise 1b and write V (verb) or A (adjective).

1 ....   5 ....
2 ....   6 ....
3 ....   7 ....
4 ....   8 ....

2 Grammar

Grammar reference: page 76

Present tense review

a Match the two parts of the sentences.

1 Janet trains at the swimming pool ☐
2 Does the gym open ☐
3 I've never ridden a skateboard ☐
4 My parents are playing tennis ☐
5 I usually go to bed ☐
6 Mr Brown has taught at this school ☐
7 Are you learning to do capoeira ☐
8 James has been to the health club ☐

A before midnight.
B now?
C at the moment.
D three times.
E every weekend.
F for nine years.
G on Sundays?
H in my life.

b (Circle) the correct words.

1 The shop *closes / is closing* at 6pm every evening.

2 *We're living / We've lived* in this flat since 2006.

3 Sarah *does / is doing* her university exams this week.

4 How long *are you / have you been* in the school orchestra?

5 I can see Pete at the bus stop. Where *does he go / is he going*?

6 I *don't speak / haven't spoken* to Paul for a long time.

7 My sister *wants / is wanting* to learn to play the drums.

c 🔊 2 Complete the dialogue with the correct form of the verbs. Then listen and check.

A: Hi, Amira. What [1]................... you .... (do)?

B: I [2]... (watch) this video on YouTube. [3]................... you .... (see) it?

A: No, I haven't. Who's the singer?

B: Someone called Lena Roth. I [4]... (not know) anything about her.

A: She [5]... (wear) a great dress.

B: Yes, and I [6]... (love) her voice. But I [7]... (listen) to this song three times now and I can't understand the words.

A: That's because you [8]... (not speak) German.

B: Oh! [9]................... she .... (sing) in German?

A: Yes, I [10]... (think) so.

③ Read

a Read the text and tick (✓) <u>two</u> correct answers.

The article is written for people who …

A enjoy doing exercise. ☐

B haven't done much exercise before. ☐

C want to get fit. ☐

D are making mistakes while they are exercising. ☐

Forum4Fitness

http://interactive.cambridge.org

Getting started

So you've decided it's time to get fit? You're aiming to do at least 30 minutes of physical exercise five days a week? Great! But if you've never done much exercise, you probably aren't sure how to begin. Here are some useful tips.

● Beginners often try to do too much too soon. Start with an activity like walking, which makes your heart beat a bit faster. Do it for about ten minutes at first and then add a few minutes every day. When you can do this easily for 30 minutes, you can start doing more energetic activities.

● Keeping fit depends on getting into a routine. Make a plan so that exercise becomes a part of your daily life. Choose activities that you enjoy (for example, swimming, cycling or playing basketball with friends) and do them regularly.

● Warming up for 5–10 minutes is very important. It slowly raises your temperature and prepares your body for more energetic physical exercise. Also, follow your work-out with some light exercises and stretching to cool down. This really helps your body to become more flexible.

● People often hope to lose weight and get more energy after the first week of exercise. Don't be disappointed when this doesn't happen! At first, you'll feel more tired than usual and you won't lose any weight, but this is normal. Remember, it takes weeks, sometimes even months, to get the best results from a new exercise programme.

b Are the sentences *right* (✓) or *wrong* (✗)?

1 The writer is giving advice for starting an exercise programme. ☐

2 At first, you should exercise for half an hour every day. ☐

3 While you are exercising, your heart beats more quickly than usual. ☐

4 Everyone should swim, ride a bike or play basketball. ☐

5 A warm-up helps your body to get warm very quickly. ☐

6 People immediately feel more energetic when they first start exercising. ☐

(4) Grammar Grammar reference: page 78

Past tense review

a Choose the correct answer: A, B or C.

I'm not very interested in skateboarding now, but I ¹_____ it when I was younger. I ²_____ a skateboard for my twelfth birthday and I ³_____ to practise every day in the skate park. One day while ⁴_____ across the bridge towards the park, I decided to practise a few moves. There weren't any people on the bridge and I ⁵_____ anyone ⁶_____ me. So I tried a few jumps and spins, but I wasn't very good. When I landed badly, the skateboard ⁷_____ off the bridge into the river. Luckily, my two older brothers ⁸_____ for me in the park. One of them went into the water and ⁹_____ my board, but after that it didn't work very well and I lost interest. These days I prefer other activities, like water skiing and team sports.

1	**A** love	**B** used to love	**C** was loving
2	**A** was getting	**B** used to get	**C** got
3	**A** use	**B** used	**C** was using
4	**A** I was walking	**B** I walked	**C** I've walked
5	**A** didn't think	**B** wasn't thinking	**C** didn't use to think
6	**A** watches	**B** watched	**C** was watching
7	**A** flew	**B** was flying	**C** used to fly
8	**A** are waiting	**B** have waited	**C** were waiting
9	**A** find	**B** found	**C** founded

b There is a mistake in each of these sentences. ~~Cross out~~ the wrong word(s) and write the correct word(s).

1 Why you were late for school yesterday?
....

2 Eva was losing her purse while she was waiting for the bus.
....

3 Where did they used to live before they moved to this town?
....

4 We couldn't use our laptops while the plane took off.
....

5 Patrick wasn't used to like jazz, but he enjoys it now.
....

6 A lot of students failed the exam because they weren't understanding the questions.
....

7 I got home at 10:30 last night. I was having a shower and then I went to bed.
....

8 What time the film began yesterday?
....

Help yourself!

Auxiliary verbs

Remember that auxiliary verbs are forms of *be*, *do* and *have* and they 'help' the main verb in a sentence. These words are very important in English.

Complete the verbs in sentences 1–5 with auxiliaries from the box.

am	are	aren't	is	isn't
were	weren't	was	wasn't	
do	don't	does	doesn't	
did	didn't			
have	haven't	has	hasn't	

1 Sorry! I _____ ring you last night because my phone _____ working.

2 _____ you tasted this dessert? I _____ think it's very nice.

3 What _____ Melanie doing at the moment? _____ she want to go shopping with us?

4 _____ Andrew and Ben find you yesterday? They _____ looking for you all afternoon.

5 My brothers _____ planning a trip to Italy and Greece now. They _____ travelled before, so they're very excited.

(5) Vocabulary

Phrasal verbs and expressions with *get*

a Complete the sentences with *get* and the words in the box.

out of	across	with	into	on	through

1 Please stop talking and .... on .... your work!
2 I'd like to stay at home this evening, but I've made an arrangement to meet Frank and I can't .... it.
3 We .... very well with our neighbours. They're really nice people.
4 This is a long book and it isn't easy to read. I don't know if I'll .... it for Monday.
5 Jill is hoping to .... college to do an Art course, but it depends on her exam results.
6 I tried to explain the idea, but it was difficult to .... the meaning .... to people.

b Complete the sentences. Use words from both boxes.

got	got	getting	get	gets	to get		home	cold	to Liverpool	some new trainers	85%	ready

1 Come on, Lisa! You have .... for school.

2 I need to ....

3 There's a train that .... at 4:45.

4 I .... in my English exam!

5 Mum's angry because I .... late last night.

6 Lisa! Your dinner's ....

(6) Pronunciation

/ɪz/

a 🔊 3 Listen and tick (✓) the word you hear.

1	☐ glass	☐ glasses
2	☐ web page	☐ web pages
3	☐ sandwich	☐ sandwiches
4	☐ Louise	☐ Louise's
5	☐ noise	☐ noises
6	☐ stretch	☐ stretches
7	☐ practise	☐ practises
8	☐ finish	☐ finishes
9	☐ change	☐ changes
10	☐ relax	☐ relaxes

b 🔊 4 Underline the words with the /ɪz/ ending. Then listen, check and repeat.

1 towns and villages
2 sandwiches and cakes
3 Max's sunglasses
4 Sam's doing his exercises
5 He washes his wife's clothes.
6 She receives emails and text messages.

c 🔊 **5** Listen and repeat the sentences.

Louise's sister speaks six languages.

Sports fans pay high prices at football matches.

Mr Davis's company makes bags and suitcases.

She stretches to warm up before she starts her exercises.

(7) Listen

a 🔊 **7** Listen to Adam and Carla talking about exercise. What sports do they do? Write *A* (Adam) and *C* (Carla) in the boxes.

b 🔊 **7** Listen again and complete the table with the types of exercise each person did last week.

Name	Monday	Tuesday	Wednesday	Thursday	Friday
Adam					
Carla					

Portfolio 1

Think about the last three days. What healthy activities did you do? Did you do anything that was not so good for your health? Write three paragraphs in a 'health diary'.

Paragraph 1

On Monday … / Three days ago …

Paragraph 2

The day before yesterday …

Paragraph 3

Yesterday …

Think about:

- exercise and sport
- other physical activities (e.g. housework, dancing, taking the dog for a walk)
- food and drink
- sleep

For each day, give yourself a score from 1 to 5 (1 = *unhealthy*, 5 = *very healthy*).

Quiz 1

a What do you remember about Unit 1? Answer all the questions you can and then check in the Student's Book.

1 Which country does the activity in picture A come from?

....

2 Are these words nouns or verbs? Write **N** or **V**.

A hide .... **B** slave ....
C belief .... **D** define ....

3 Look at picture B. ~~Cross out~~ the sentence which is wrong.

A These people only perform in China.
B Matthew Ahmet joined them when he was 17.
C He trained with them in China.

4 Circle the words which are martial arts.

judo   tennis   aerobics   capoeira
belly dancing   fitness

5 Circle the correct words.

I'm more *energy / energetic* and my back and shoulders are more *flexible / flexibility* since I started my exercise *event / class*.

6 There are two mistakes in this sentence. Write the correct sentence.

Jack doesn't do athletics before but he's wanting to learn and he's training hard now.

....
....

7 Complete the table.

Verb	Past simple	Past participle
A take	....	....
B become	....	....
C get	....	....

8 Complete the sentences with the correct form of the verbs.

Mum always .... (make) her own pasta now. She and Dad .... (not eat) pasta in the past, but they .... (get) interested in it last year while they .... (travel) in Italy.

9 Circle the correct words.

I get *out of / on with / through to* my cousin and I hope we get *through to / into / across* the same university.

10 Tick (✓) the words that end in the sound /ɪz/.
manages ☐   tastes ☐   catches ☐
offices ☐   Mike's ☐

b 🔊 8 Listen and check your answers.

c Now look at your Student's Book and write three more quiz questions for Unit 1.

Question: ....
....
Answer: ....

Question: ....
....
Answer: ....

Question: ....
....
Answer: ....

2 Waste not, want not

1 Vocabulary

Electrical items

a Add vowels (*a*, *e*, *i*, *o*, *u*) to make words for electrical items and match them with the pictures.

1	tstr	*toaster*	G
2	wshng mchn		
3	mcrwv		
4	hrdryr		
5	vcm clnr		
6	frzr		
7	fd prcssr		
8	dshwshr		
9	lctrc rzr		
10	tmbl dryr		

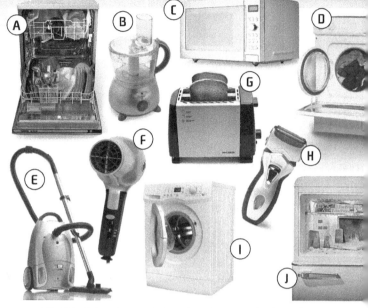

b Write definitions for the words in Exercise 1a. Use the words in the table.

for cleaning	hair.
to make	food.
for cooking	the floor.
for removing	plates, cutlery, etc.
to dry	toast.
to keep food	clothes.
for preparing	very cold.

1 *A toaster is used to make toast.*
2
3
4
5
6
7
8
9
10

Help yourself!

Verb + -*er* and -*or*

A lot of nouns are formed by verb + -*er* or -*or*.

clean + -*er*	**cleaner**	(= someone/something that cleans)
freeze + -*er*	**freezer**	(= something that freezes)
visit + -*or*	**visitor**	(= someone who visits)

Write the names of these objects using the verbs in the box. Use a dictionary when you need to, and check if the ending is -*er* or -*or*.

speak   print   mix   calculate   cook   radiate

1		4	
2		5	
3		6	

Add these words to the list of electrical items in your notebook.

② Grammar Grammar reference: page 76

Present perfect with *just*/*yet*/*already*

a Write the sentences in the present perfect.

1 They / record / a new song – just

They've just recorded a new song.

2 you / finish / your homework? – yet

....

3 I / hear / this song – already

....

4 Robbie / repair / his motorbike – already

....

5 We / not have / lunch – yet

....

6 I / put / the plates in the dishwasher – just

....

7 Isobel / book / her flight to Athens? – yet

....

b 🔊 9 Write sentences. Use the present perfect form of the verbs with *just*, *yet* or *already*. Then listen and check.

be	see	tell	miss	~~get~~	get	not speak
not give	not see					

¹I / a text message from Danny. ²He / the train.

1 *I've just got a text message from Danny.*

2 ....

³We / here for 40 minutes! ⁴You / us the menu.

3 ....

4 ....

Clara: Let's watch this. ⁵I / it.

Josh: Oh no, not again! ⁶I / it twice.

5 ....

6 ....

Tom: ⁷you / Sofia about the concert?

Anna: ⁸No, she / home. ⁹I / to her.

7 ....

8 ....

9 ....

③ Pronunciation

Stress patterns

a 🔊 10 Draw a line between the two syllables in these words. Then listen and <u>underline</u> the stressed syllable. Listen again and repeat.

be|lief   fitness   inspire   recent
metal   escaped   level   relaxed

b 🔊 11 Draw lines between the three syllables. <u>Underline</u> the stressed syllable. Then listen, check and repeat.

expensive   disappear   sunglasses
develop   overweight   energy   director
flexible   millionaire

c 🔊 12 Draw lines between the four syllables. <u>Underline</u> the stressed syllable. Then listen, check and repeat.

introduction   definitely   electrical
supermodel   technology   helicopter
disappointed   intelligent   independent

Practise saying these words

🔊 **13** average   dishwasher   electrical
environment   freezer   government
microwave   poisonous   razor   recycle
underground   vacuum cleaner

④ Listen

a   🔊 **14** Alice and her brother Jamie
are having a party tonight for a friend's
birthday. Listen and tick (✓) the electrical
items you hear.

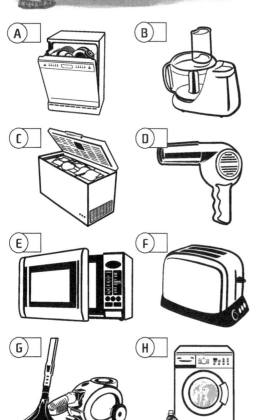

(A)   (B)

(C)   (D)

(E)   (F)

(G)   (H)

b   🔊 **14** Listen again and complete the sentences.

Jamie hasn't finished cleaning the ¹............................
yet. He's already done the shopping at the
²............................ . There are some pizzas in the
³............................ and the ⁴............................ are
in the fridge. Alice has just finished mixing the
⁵............................ but she hasn't ⁶............................
it yet. Jamie's ⁷............................ isn't ready to wear.
He's going to put it in the ⁸............................ .

⑤ Vocabulary

Prefixes

a   Complete the words with the correct prefix: *re-*,
over-, *under-* or *pre-*.

1   I've started an exercise programme because I'm
....................weight.

2   ....heat the oven to 180° and cook the meat
for 40 minutes.

3   Doctors earn a lot of money but nurses are
....................paid.

4   Metal from old machines can be ....used to
make new products.

5   At the bottom of the building there's an
....................ground car park.

6   I want to ....take my French exam because I
got a really bad mark in it.

7   I'm not going to buy these shoes. They're nice, but
they're ....priced.

8   My travel card for the bus is ....paid. I put
more money on the card online when I need to.

b   One word is wrong in each of these sentences.
~~Cross out~~ the mistake and write the correct word.

1   I'm retaking the batteries for my camera.

....

2   We can't get into that club because we're
underground.

....

3   Gisele Bündchen is a superpower. She's earned
millions of dollars for her magazine photos.

....

4   I missed my bus this morning because I overpriced.

....

5   When I get home late from work I buy a pre-paid meal
and heat it up in the microwave.

....

6   The Metro in Paris is an under-age railway.

....

c Write true answers, using your own ideas.

1 a type of food that is precooked when you buy it ....
2 something you can find underground ....
3 something that you think is overpriced ....
4 two countries which are superpowers ....
5 a job that you think is underpaid ....
6 a film star who is overweight ....
7 an item you can recharge ....

6 Grammar Grammar reference: page 78

Present perfect continuous

a Complete the sentences with the verbs in the present perfect continuous.

> **Check it out!**
>
> The present perfect continuous is similar to the present perfect simple, but it always expresses the idea that the action has continued for some time.

1 We won't be able to play today. It .... (rain) all morning.

2 You should get some exercise. You .... (sit) there since breakfast time.

3 Megan has got a job in the garden centre. She .... (work) there for a month.

4 The match has already started. They .... (play) for ten minutes.

5 He should stop and have a rest. He .... (drive) for five hours.

6 Ben is one of my friends on Facebook. We .... (write) to each other since we were 14 years old.

b Complete the dialogues. Use the present perfect continuous form of the verbs in the box.

> enjoy   have   study   watch   do   learn
> not wait   not practise

1 A: Sorry I'm late!
   B: That's OK. We .... long.

2 A: What .... you .... lately?
   B: Nothing much. I .... for my exams.

3 A: The band doesn't sound very good, does it?
   B: No. That's because they .... lately.

4 A: .... you .... *Friends and Families* on Channel 3?
   B: Yes, we .... it a lot.

5 A: How long .... Sam .... to play the violin?
   B: He .... lessons since September.

(7) Read

a Read the web page. What topic do the news items share?

1 recycling ☐   **2** reducing waste ☐   **3** saving money ☐

GoGreen

http://interactive.cambridge.org

What's new on the green scene?

Volunteers from a group called EcoFriends are trying to reduce the waste created by bottled water. They have been inviting people to take a 'tap water test' and have found that most people can't taste any difference between tap water and bottled water. 'Tap water tastes just as good and it doesn't create any waste,' says organiser John. 'And it only costs one penny per litre, so you save money too.'

This year the organisers of the Glastonbury Music Festival are collecting used batteries and electrical waste for recycling. The festival has been recycling other waste for some time. There are 15,000 bins for different materials on the festival site and over 1,000 tonnes of waste are recycled.

Students at 40 schools in London have been taking part in a recycling programme for the past year. They have helped to recycle 80 tonnes of cardboard and food waste, which would normally go into landfills. The food is recycled using a new process called anaerobic digestion. Heating breaks down the food to form a 'biogas' which generates electricity for hundreds of homes.

A survey shows that the use of plastic bags in UK supermarkets has dropped by over four billion in the past four years. Shoppers have been bringing their own shopping bags or using old plastic bags. These results are good, but there's still a long way to go. Plastic bags are one of the worst products of the throw-away society and more than a trillion are made worldwide every year.

---

b Choose the correct answer: A, B or C.

1 The members of EcoFriends
 A want to save water.
 B want people to drink tap water.
 C want people to recycle their bottles.

2 They have been doing the 'tap water test' to show that bottled water
 A doesn't taste very good.
 B doesn't have a better taste than tap water.
 C is more expensive than tap water.

3 Forty London schools
 A started the recycling programme a year ago.
 B finished their recycling programme a year ago.
 C have taken a lot of rubbish to landfill sites.

4 The Glastonbury Festival
 A hasn't done much recycling yet.
 B has already recycled a lot of rubbish.
 C has just started recycling rubbish.

5 In supermarkets in the UK, customers
 A have stopped using plastic bags.
 B have used 4 billion plastic bags in four years.
 C haven't been using so many plastic bags recently.

Portfolio 2

Imagine your friend has moved to another town. Write an email giving him/her your news.

Paragraph 1
What have you been doing lately? Think about:
• your school life   • your social life

Paragraph 2
What have other people been doing? Think about:
• your friends   • your family

Paragraph 3
What's been happening in your town or neighbourhood? Think about:
• recent events   • changes that have taken place

Check it out!

If you are describing an event that happened at a particular time in the past, use the past simple, not the present perfect.
*We've been preparing for the school play and <u>last Tuesday</u> we **tried** on our costumes for the first time.*

Quiz (2)

a What do you remember about Unit 2? Answer all the questions you can and then check in the Student's Book.

1 What's the name of the sculpture in picture A?

....

2 How many electrical items does the average family own in the UK?

10 ☐   20 ☐   25 ☐

3 (Circle) the odd one out.

toaster   food processor
microwave   dishwasher

4 Match the words to make four electrical items.

electric   tumble   machine   cleaner
vacuum   washing   dryer   razor

....
....

5 Use *yet, just* and *already* in this dialogue.

A: I've ¹............... seen Ella. She's in the café.

B: Has she been to the gym ²............... ?

A: Yes, she's ³............... had a work-out this morning.

6 If food is *overcooked*, this means that

A it isn't cooked enough.   ☐
B it is cooked too much.   ☐
C it is cooked better than usual.   ☐

7 Match the words with the definitions.

1 remake   **A** a very famous performer
2 underwater   **B** to create something again
3 superstar   **C** below the surface of the sea, a river, a pool, etc.

8 (Circle) the correct word.

We've been waiting here *for / since* 20 minutes.

9 Look at picture B and complete the dialogue. Write one word in each gap.

A: .... he just ....
   .... ?

B: Yes, he ....

10 Match the words with the stress patterns.

1 ●•   **A** microwave
2 •●   **B** vacuum
3 ●••   **C** container
4 •●•   **D** reduce

b 🔊 15 Listen and check your answers.

c Now look at your Student's Book and write three more quiz questions for Unit 2.

Question: ....
....
Answer: ....

Question: ....
....
Answer: ....

Question: ....
....
Answer: ....

3 Forces of nature

1 Vocabulary

Natural disasters

a Write words 1–7 in the puzzle. Then use the ◯ letters to make one more word for a natural disaster.

1
2
3
4
5
6
7

b Read the descriptions and write the words from Exercise 1a.

1 There has been almost no rain here for the past three years.

....

2 Snow and ice rolled down the mountain at incredible speed.

....

3 There was so much rain that many houses were under water.

....

4 The largest wave was over ten metres high and it travelled at 800km per hour across the ocean.

....

5 The ground shook for 30 seconds. In that time many buildings were badly damaged.

....

6 We've had temperatures of around 35°C every day this week.

....

7 When it came in from the sea, the wind was blowing at 120km per hour.

....

8 Smoke was pouring from the mountain and it threw out a rain of red-hot rock.

....

Help yourself!

Idioms: the weather

Read these sentences. Then match the weather idioms in **bold** with the definitions.

1 Everyone was really upset about the decision at first, but it was just **a storm in a teacup**. ☐

2 I can't go out at all this weekend. I'm **snowed under** with homework. ☐

3 Monday seemed like a normal day, but it was just **the calm before the storm**. On Tuesday everything went wrong! ☐

4 Are you OK? You're looking a bit **under the weather**. ☐

5 It's been a really awful week, but I think we've managed to **weather the storm**. ☐

6 They **blow hot and cold** about the plan. I don't know what they'll decide to do. ☐

A to get through a difficult time successfully

B to have opinions or feelings that keep changing – sometimes positive, sometimes negative

C having a huge amount of work to do

D a small problem which people think is a lot more important than it really is

E not feeling very well

F a quiet period before big problems arrive

2 Grammar

Grammar reference: page 82

will and *going to*

a (Circle) the correct words.

1 I've ordered a special software program on the internet.
I'll / I'm going to use it for writing music.

2 A: Is that the phone?
B: Don't worry, *I'll / I'm going to* answer it.

3 A: You've got a great voice. Why don't you join the school choir?
B: Mmm … maybe. *I'll / I'm going to* think about it.

Check it out!

If a decision has already been made, use *going to*. If a decision is made at the time of speaking, use *will*.

4 A: Don't forget your camera.
B: Oh, it's not working very well, so *I won't / I'm not going to* take it.

5 A: Where *will you / are you going to* meet your friends?
B: In front of the theatre.

6 A: I'm having a party for Helen, but I want it to be a surprise.
B: Oh, OK. We *won't / aren't going to* say anything about it.

b Complete the sentences. Use the correct form of *will* or *going to*.

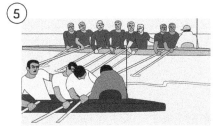

1 Listen to this song. I think you .... (like) it.

2 I'd love to go, but I probably .... (not have) enough money.

3 Look! It .... (land) on the roof.

4 What .... you .... (do) with that?

5 They're faster than us. We .... (not win).

6 Maybe we .... (be) rich and famous one day.

Check it out!

Will and *going to* are both used for predictions, and often both forms are correct. But we normally use *going to* if the prediction is a sure conclusion based on strong evidence.

c 🔊 16 Complete the dialogues with <u>one or two</u> words. Then listen and check.

A: The hurricane ¹................................ to hit land some time tonight. We're ²................................ sleep in the basement. It's the safest place in the house.

B: When ³................................ be safe to come out?

A: I don't know. But they say the winds ⁴................................ be very strong, so we ⁵................................ to move until we hear on the radio that everything's OK.

A: I'm ⁶................................ to do any work this afternoon. It's too hot.

B: Yes, I know. It's hard to do anything in this heat wave. How long is ⁷................................ to last?

A: For the whole week. They say the weather ⁸................................ get cooler until Sunday.

B: Well, I think ⁹................................ have a swim.

A: Good idea. ¹⁰................................ come with you.

③ Read

a Read the four answers to questions about volcanoes. Match the answers with the questions (A–D).

A Which volcano is going to produce the next big eruption?

B What information do volcanologists look for?

C What was the worst volcanic disaster in human history?

D Will these volcanoes erupt again?

Volcanoes FAQs

1 ....

Santorini (Greece, 1630 BC) and Krakatoa (Indonesia, 1883) are probably the best known. When these volcanic islands exploded, they created huge waves of hot gas and rock and giant tsunamis. But the 1815 eruption of Mount Tambora in Indonesia was worse. 160km^3 of volcanic material shot into the air, and the whole mountain was described as 'a mass of liquid fire'. Ash covered the land for hundreds of kilometres and hid the sun. Across the world, the temperature dropped and 1816 was called 'the year without a summer'. About 72,000 people died, many of them from hunger, as a result of this eruption.

2 ....

Yes, Tambora, Santorini and Krakatoa are all still active. In fact Krakatoa is pushing up a new volcanic island, called Anak Krakatoa (Child of Krakatoa), which is growing fast. Experts say that all three volcanoes will definitely produce big eruptions again – but they won't happen soon.

3 ....

Nobody knows. The greatest danger will probably come from the area around the Pacific Ocean, called the Pacific Ring of Fire, where most of the world's active volcanoes are found. Some, like Popocatépetl in Mexico, are close to big cities, while others, like Merapi in Indonesia, are extremely active and have already caused recent disasters. Volcanologists are carefully watching many of the volcanoes in this region.

4 ....

They find out how often earthquakes take place and look for changes in the shape of the mountain. They also check for increases in temperature and changes in the gases coming out. These can be signs that the volcano is going to erupt. But it is impossible to predict exactly where or when an eruption will happen or how large it will be.

b Are the sentences *right* (✓) or *wrong* (✗)?

1 The Santorini and Krakatoa eruptions were the worst in human history. ☐

2 The Earth's climate became colder because of the Tambora eruption. ☐

3 Tambora probably won't erupt again in the future. ☐

4 If Popocatépetl has a big eruption, it will affect a large number of people. ☐

5 Experts are going to start checking volcanoes in the Pacific Ring of Fire. ☐

6 Scientists can't be sure when a volcano is going to erupt. ☐

④ Vocabulary

Outdoor equipment

a Put the letters in order and write the words.

skuccark	soglegg	sicten letpelner	karano	nus remac
elfece	pigleens gab	utiwest	throc	nagwilk stobo

1 two things that you wear to keep warm

....

2 two things that you put on your skin for protection

....

3 two things that you wear in the water

....

4 something that you carry on your back

....

5 something that you lie in when you're in a tent

....

6 something that creates light so you can see at night

....

7 something that you wear on your feet

....

b Complete the sentences with words from Exercise 4a.

1 You need a good pair of .... when you go trekking.

2 Professional swimmers wear .... to protect their eyes in the swimming pool.

3 It's too dark to see where we're going. We need a ....

4 I'm going to carry everything for the camping trip in my ....

5 We must remember to take some .... The mosquitoes are bad at this time of year.

6 I slept well while I was camping because I've got a nice warm ....

7 Always put some .... on for your skin when you're sunbathing.

8 Jack wears a .... when he goes surfing in cold weather.

5 Grammar Grammar reference: page 84

Future continuous

a Match the sentences.

1 At 4:30 this afternoon I'll be in town. ☐

2 This time next week the school will be closed. ☐

3 Alice will be on the ferry this evening. ☐

4 I hope Leah will ring me tonight. ☐

5 Between 12:30 and 1:30 Janet will be in the school dining room. ☐

6 We'll be in the music room for an hour after school today. ☐

A She'll be having her lunch.

B We'll be practising for the concert.

C I'll be waiting for her call.

D We'll be having a good time on holiday.

E I'll be shopping for clothes.

F She won't be travelling by plane.

b Write your own answers to these questions.

1 What will you be doing in two hours' time?

....

2 What will you be doing this time tomorrow?

....

3 What will you be doing at 9pm this evening?

....

4 What will be happening in your home at 8am on Sunday?

....

....

c Complete the dialogue. Use the future continuous form of the verbs.

ride	get	do	shine	look	surf
not think		not sit			

A: The long weekend's coming up! What ^{1}................ you .... this time on Saturday?

B: Well, I certainly ^{2}................ here at my desk. I ^{3}................ at Pearl Beach with my friend Max. I can see it now. The sun ^{4}................ and we ^{5}................ our boards on those big blue waves. We ^{6}................ probably .... hungry and I ^{7}................ forward to a meal of fresh fish and salad at the Pearl Beach Café. I ^{8}................ about school work, that's for sure!

6 Pronunciation

/uː/ and /ʊ/

a 🔊 17 Listen and tick (✓) the correct vowel sound.

	/uː/	/ʊ/
1 room	☐	☐
2 took	☐	☐
3 foot	☐	☐
4 pool	☐	☐
5 soon	☐	☐
6 stood	☐	☐
7 roof	☐	☐
8 cook	☐	☐

b 🔊 **18** Find a way through the puzzle. Follow the words which have the /uː/ sound. Then listen, check and repeat.

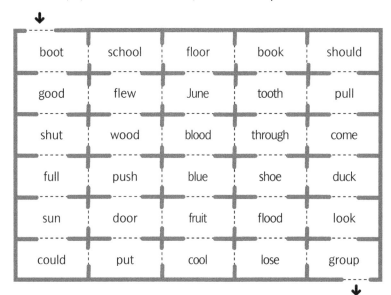

boot	school	floor	book	should
good	flew	June	tooth	pull
shut	wood	blood	through	come
full	push	blue	shoe	duck
sun	door	fruit	flood	look
could	put	cool	lose	group

c 🔊 **19** Listen and practise saying these sentences.

Those new boots look cool!
There's some good food in Julia's cookery book.
You should put on some waterproof shoes.

Practise saying these words

🔊 **20** avalanche　drought earthquake　emergency　huge hurricane　necessary　rucksack successfully　tornado

7 Listen

a 🔊 **21** Jess and Emma are going on a camping trip with a group of friends. Listen and tick (✓) the picture that shows the place where they are going to stay.

(A)

(B)

(C)

b 🔊 **21** Listen again and answer the questions.

1 What will the weather be like
　a on Saturday? ....
　b on Sunday? ....
2 What clothes are they going to take?
....
....
....
3 Why will the water be too cold for swimming?
....
....
4 What is Emma going to bring?
....
5 What is Jess going to buy tomorrow?
....
....
6 Which of the two girls do you think is going to this campsite for the first time?
....

Portfolio 3

You have written an email to a friend to say that you are planning a beach barbecue, and you receive this answer. Write a reply answering your friend's questions.

Your idea for a barbecue on the beach sounds great. Give me some more info. When are you having it, and where, exactly? Who else is coming and how are we going to get there? What about food – is everyone going to bring something? I'll bring a dessert if you like. Are you going to organise some music? Also, what are you going to wear? Let me know!

Quiz 3

A
B

a What do you remember about Unit 3? Answer all the questions you can and then check in the Student's Book.

1 **What is the nationality of the person who wrote this?**

In Victoria we often get heat waves in January and February.

....

2 **What is the name of the heavy rain that comes to India every year?**

....

3 **What is the word for the extreme weather in picture A?**

....

4 **Find the words for three natural disasters in this puzzle.**

e h d t u r s c r o u n u n a g a r h m i t i

....

5 ~~Cross out~~ the verb that is not correct in each sentence.

A The weather	will get is getting is going to get	better soon.
B My parents	won't work aren't working aren't going to work	tomorrow.

6 The man in picture B is wearing
.... and a
....

7 **One word is wrong in each sentence. ~~Cross it out~~ and write the correct word.**

a I'm going to put my sleeping sack in the tent. ....

b Take some insect cream for the mosquitoes. ....

c He's going to buy a new pair of walking bags. ....

8 **Complete the sentences. Use the future continuous.**

A: ....
(you / stay) in Rome on 10 March?

B: No, ...
(I / not travel) in Italy then.

9 Match the words in the boxes to make four time expressions.

at in on	Wednesday morning
tomorrow	half past six the evening

....

....

10 **Which vowel sound is the odd one out?**

A book   good   cool

B wood   spoon   food

C room   flood   pool

b 🔊 22 Listen and check your answers.

c Now look at your Student's Book and write three more quiz questions for Unit 3.

Question: ....

....

Answer: ....

Question: ....

....

Answer: ....

Question: ....

....

Answer: ....

4 Friends 4ever

1 Vocabulary

Friendship

a Make six sentences from the table and match them with the pictures.

She's having an	up	with her.
Sam let	~~on~~	with her boyfriend.
Hannah has fallen	us	with each other.
~~He gets~~	cross	Eduardo.
I was really	out with	~~well with everyone.~~
They've made	argument	down tonight.

1 Matthew has lots of friends. ~~He gets on well with everyone.~~ [picture ..C..]

2 My sister borrowed my sunglasses and broke them. ....
[picture ....]

3 A: Who's making all that noise?
B: It's Annie. ....
[picture ....]

4 They aren't arguing now.
....
[picture ....]

5 ....
They haven't spoken to each other since Friday.
[picture ....]

6 ....
We had to play without a drummer.
[picture ....]

b There is a mistake in each of these sentences. ~~Cross out~~ the wrong word and write the correct word.

1 It's important to stick out for your friends if they're in trouble. ....

2 They got up after their argument, so they're good friends again now. ....

3 I get in well with most people in my class.
....

4 If you don't stop copying my work, I'll tell about you. ....

5 Calm down! I don't want to make an argument with you. ....

6 Don't worry about Kate – she won't let us up.
....

Help yourself!

Friendship: more phrasal verbs

Read the verbs and definitions. Then complete the sentences.

get together	to meet by arrangement
come over	to come to my home
drop in (on someone)	to visit (someone) informally, without an invitation
run into someone	to meet someone unexpectedly
count on someone	to depend on someone and expect them to do the right thing
hit it off (with someone)	to form a friendship (with someone) immediately

1 I think I'll .... on Erica on my way home.

2 I haven't seen you for ages! Let's .... next week.

3 I've always got on really well with Jack. We .... as soon as we met.

4 You can always .... Hassan. He never lets you down.

5 I was shopping at the market this morning when I .... Natalie.

6 I'm not going out this afternoon. Mick and Laura are going to .... to watch the football.

② Listen

a 🔊 **23** Listen to the dialogues (1–3) and match them with the photos.

(A)

(B)

(C)

b 🔊 **23** Listen again. Are the sentences *right* (✓), *wrong* (✗) or *doesn't say* (–)?

1 Greg and Tony
   a are cross with each other. ☐
   b are making up after an argument. ☐
   c have been friends for a long time. ☐

2 Kelly is
   a telling on Julie. ☐
   b having an argument with Mr Thomas. ☐
   c sticking up for her friend. ☐

3 Steve and David
   a are mates who share a flat. ☐
   b don't usually get on well. ☐
   c never argue. ☐

③ Grammar Grammar reference: page 84

if, when, as soon as and unless

a Match the two parts of the sentences.

1 We'll open the windows ☐
2 I'll pay you back ☐
3 I'll be there at about 10 o'clock ☐
4 My brother will be happy ☐
5 The file will start downloading ☐
6 I won't be able to carry this ☐
7 We'll have to leave ☐
8 You won't get good results ☐

A if you click on 'OK'.
B when it cools down outside.
C unless somebody helps me.
D as soon as I can.
E unless you try hard.
F as soon as the taxi arrives.
G when the football season begins.
H if the train is on time.

b Complete the sentences. Use *if*, *when*, *as soon as* or *unless* and the correct form of the verbs.

1 Lisa's boyfriend will meet her .... she .... (get) to the station.

2 These plants will die .... it .... (not rain) soon.

3 You .... (not be) able to find the campsite .... you follow the map carefully.

4 Look, it's really late. We'll have to go to bed .... the film .... (finish).

5 .... there .... (be) some nice strawberries at the market, I'll get some for dessert.

6 I can't wait to see you! I'll come and see you .... you .... (arrive).

7 Tim will probably do a course in conservation .... he .... (leave) school.

8 .... the weather is bad, we .... (have) lunch outside at the café.

4 Vocabulary

Adjectives of personality

a Look at the table: 3 is H, 4 is E and 5 is L. Write all these letters in the puzzle. Then complete the personality adjectives and write the letters in the table.

1	2	3	4	5	6	7	8	9	10
		H	E	L					

11	12	13	14	15	16	17	18	19	20

b Complete the table of opposites with adjectives from Exercise 4a.

Adjective	Opposite
1	quiet
2	rude
3	boring, uninteresting
4	shy and unsociable
5	anxious, stressed
6	insensitive, hard-hearted
7	respectful
8	easy-going and cheerful

c Complete the sentences with adjectives from Exercise 4a.

1 Karen doesn't worry about anything. She's always relaxed and ....

2 It's important to be .... when you're meeting an older person for the first time.

3 Our neighbour really loves talking. She's a very .... person.

4 Don't sit at home! If you want to make new friends, you should try to be more ....

5 Evan is always .... when anyone has a problem. He really understands how people feel.

6 I try to be .... at home. When Mum's cooking or doing the housework, I don't mind doing it with her.

7 She didn't say 'thank you' for her birthday present. She's so .... !

8 Dan is sometimes .... in class so the teachers get a bit angry with him.

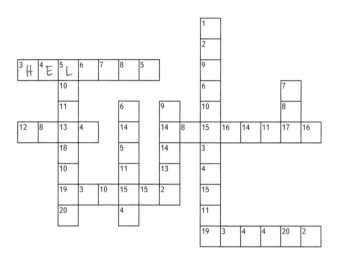

5 Pronunciation

Friendly intonation

a 🔊 24 Listen and read. Is the relationship friendly (*F*) or polite (*P*)? Then listen again and repeat.

1 A: Is there anything else you need?
  B: No, that's fine. Thanks a lot for your help. ☐

2 A: Sorry, I'm not going to be able to come on Friday.
  B: Oh, that's disappointing. ☐

3 A: Thanks for a really nice evening. It was excellent.
  B: Well, I'm glad you enjoyed it. ☐

4 A: A parcel has just arrived for you.
  B: Oh, good. I've been expecting it. ☐

b 🔊 25 Listen and tick (✓) the sentence if you think the relationship is friendly. Then listen again and repeat.

1 Goodbye. Have a good trip. ☐
2 Right, then. I'll see you at four o'clock tomorrow. ☐
3 Could you come here for a minute, please? ☐
4 You should get some sleep now. You look tired. ☐
5 Sorry. I can't help you at the moment. ☐

Practise saying these words

🔊 26 angry annoyed argument audience career cheeky entertainer humour moody occasionally support sympathetic

---

6 Grammar Grammar reference: page 86

First and second conditional review

a Complete the sentences with the correct form of the verbs in the box.

meet	be	do	can	respect	not call	not be

1 I .... able to find out about the concert if I look on the internet.

2 If Ellie .... me this evening, I'll be annoyed.

3 I'd buy one of those jumpers if they .... so expensive.

4 What .... you .... if you lost your wallet?

Check it out!

Remember, the past tense of *can* is *could*.

*If I **could** catch the 4 o'clock train, I'd be home earlier.*

However, there is no future form of *can*. Instead, we normally use *will be able to* when referring to the future.

*You**'ll be able to** make this dessert if you follow the recipe.*

5 If Ali didn't have to study for his exams, he .... come to the cinema with us.

6 People .... you if you stick up for your beliefs.

7 If you .... our neighbour, you'd see why we find her so interesting.

b Write sentences. Use *if* and the first or second conditional.

1 the bus / not come / soon – we / be / late

....
....

2 this pizza / taste / better – it / have / more cheese on it

....
....

3 I / can / ride – I / go / with them

....
....

4 you / use / this – the mosquitoes / not bite / you

....
....

5 what / we / do – it / rain ?

....

6 he / not get on / well with children – he / not be / such a good teacher

....
....

c Choose two topics and write two sentences on each: a first conditional sentence and a second conditional sentence.

• your favourite band/musician   • your best friend   • a family member   • a school subject   • a job

A If Rihanna records a new album this year, it will go to number 1 in the charts.

B It would be fantastic if Rihanna gave a concert in our town.

1 A ....
   ....

   B ....
   ....

2 A ....
   ....

   B ....
   ....

(7) Read

a Read the two posts on a teen website. Why has Laila written her post?

A to tell a friend some important news ☐

B to get some advice about a problem ☐

C to give her opinion about something ☐

Laila

http://interactive.cambridge.org

Share It!

Laila

I've known my friend Holly for three years and we've shared lots of things together. But she's started to get very possessive about our friendship and this is becoming a real problem for me. She expects me to spend all my free time with her and she rings or texts me about six times a day. I get tired of this, but if I didn't answer her calls, I know she'd be hurt and angry. When I talk to other people, she's very rude to them – it's so embarrassing. If she had other mates, she wouldn't need me so much, but I can't force her to make friends with other people. I don't want to lose her friendship, but I sometimes think she won't be happy unless I cut everyone else out of my life. What can I do?

This situation won't get any better unless you take positive action. If I were you, I'd try talking to her first. Tell

Myra

her you need more space, but do this quietly and without getting cross. If she knows how you feel, perhaps she'll be able to change.

You definitely need to have other friends in your life. When you're all together, make sure you include Holly in the conversation and make her feel welcome. If you can both go out with a group, you'll have more room to breathe and she will have a chance to form other friendships too.

However, if she doesn't listen to you and keeps trying to destroy your relationships with other people, I think you should think about ending this friendship. If she was a true friend, she wouldn't want to control you or make you feel guilty about enjoying yourself. It's never OK for anyone to try to own another person and this situation will only get worse if you don't do something about it.

b Choose the correct answer: A, B or C.

1 Laila and Holly
   A are close friends.
   B have fallen out with each other.
   C have had problems for three years.

2 When Laila gets texts and calls from Holly, she
   A answers them.
   B sometimes doesn't answer them.
   C never answers them.

3 Holly
   A wants to make new friends.
   B gets embarrassed by Laila's other friends.
   C has only one friend.

4 Myra thinks that Laila
   A doesn't really have a serious problem.
   B is feeling too negative about the situation.
   C must do something about the problem.

5 She suggests that Laila should
   A talk to her other friends about Holly.
   B go out with other people.
   C avoid going out with Holly.

6 She thinks that
   A Holly will want to damage Laila's friendships.
   B Laila should stop being friends with Holly.
   C Holly might not change her behaviour.

Portfolio 4

Read about Lee's problem and write a reply giving advice. Use some of these expressions:

If you …   Why don't you …?   If I were you, …
How about ___ing …?   I (don't) think you should …

Lee I've recently moved to a new school and I need to make new friends, but I'm finding it really hard. The other kids have all known each other for years and they aren't interested in me. I've kept in touch with a few of my old friends, but we hardly ever see each other now. No one talks to me at my new school and I'm losing my self-confidence, although I pretend I'm OK. Can you help me?

Quiz 4

a What do you remember about Unit 4? Answer all the questions you can and then check in the Student's Book.

1 How did the young man in picture A meet his best friend?

....

2 What does *BAFTA* stand for?

....

3 There are three mistakes in this sentence. Cross out the wrong words and write the correct words.

Tim used to keep on well with Matthew, but they made an argument and fell off with each other three weeks ago.

....

4 Circle the correct words.

You promised to stick *up / down* for me, but you've let me *up / down*!

5 Circle the correct words.

I / I'll check my emails as soon as *I / I'll* get home.

6 Rewrite the sentence using *unless*.

We'll go to the concert if the tickets aren't too expensive.

....

7 Circle the words that could describe the girl in picture B.

annoyed   helpful   cheeky
outgoing   angry   cross

8 Match the adjectives.

1 laid-back   **A** talkative
2 rude   **B** impolite
3 chatty   **C** relaxed

9 Put the words in order and write the sentence.

doesn't / if / get inside / won't / Carlo / find / he / be able to / his key

....
....

10 Complete the sentences with the correct form of the verbs.

Cathy and I ^{1}........................... (go) swimming if it ^{2}........................... (not be) so cold today. If it ^{3}........................... (get) warmer during the week, we ^{4}........................... (go) to the beach next weekend.

b 🔊 **27** Listen and check your answers.

c Now look at your Student's Book and write three more quiz questions for Unit 4.

Question: ....
....
Answer: ....

Question: ....
....
Answer: ....

Question: ....
....
Answer: ....

5 Top of the class

1 Vocabulary

School

a Read the clues and complete the crossword.

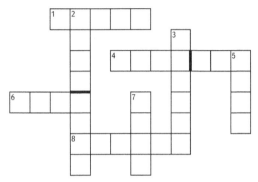

Across

1 Don't try to .... in exams. It's dishonest.
4 Ryan got 94% in the Geography test, but he didn't .... Rachel got 95%. (2 words)
6 We have a break from school at the end of every ....
8 To prepare for your exam, you need to .... the work you've done during the year.

Down

2 I'm disappointed in this result. I was hoping to get a .... in Maths. (2 words)
3 If you don't do well this time, you might have to .... the exam.
5 Harry is really good at French. He'll .... the exam easily.
7 I'm really worried about these exams. It will be awful if I .... !

b (Circle) the correct words.

1 A: Why are Paul and Amir *at / in / on* detention?
  B: Because they skived *out / away / off* after lunch yesterday.
2 Liz got 30% in her exam so she's going to *revise / retake / cheat* it.
3 Before a test, I always *pass / fail / revise* with my best friend.
4 Take care, you really need to get a *high / right / correct* mark in this exam.
5 Enzo is brilliant. He came top *in / of / on* Science and Maths again this year.

2 Grammar Grammar reference: page 90

Permission: *can, let, be allowed to*

> **Check it out!**
>
> **The verb *let* is irregular. The past simple and the past participle form is *let*.**
>
> *Mum **let** me go to the music festival last year.*
> *I've never **let** anyone read my diary.*

a Complete the sentences with the words in the box.

let	lets	allowed	is	don't	wasn't
can	can't				

1 Sorry, you .... take photos in the gallery.
2 My parents .... let me stay up late.
3 In the UK, you're .... to drive when you're 17.
4 The teachers .... us go home ten minutes early yesterday.
5 When Grandma was my age, she .... allowed to have a boyfriend.
6 I don't think you .... get into the club unless you're over 18.
7 No one .... allowed to smoke in our house.
8 My brother sometimes .... me borrow his leather jacket.

b 🔊 28 Complete the dialogues with one word for each gap. Then listen and check.

A: ¹_____ your teachers let you bring phones to school?

B: Yes, we ²_____ bring them, but we aren't ³_____ to use them in class.

A: Yeah, we have the same rule. We ⁴_____ take a phone into the classroom unless it's switched off.

A: ⁵_____ I borrow your DVD of last week's concert?

B: Yeah, sure. Didn't you watch it?

A: No. I had an argument with my father and he said I was rude to him. So he didn't let ⁶_____ watch TV and I wasn't allowed ⁷_____ record anything. He told me I ⁸_____ even play a computer game last week.

B: Oh, OK. I'll give it to you tomorrow. Will you ⁹_____ allowed to watch it then?

A: Yes, everything's OK now.

③ Listen

a 🔊 29 Listen to Martin talking about the rules at his school. Tick (✓) the topics you hear.

smoking	☐	uniform	☐
cheating	☐	homework	☐
phones	☐	sport	☐
rubbish	☐	accessories	☐
food	☐	hairstyles	☐

b 🔊 29 Listen again and look at the picture of two students in Martin's school. Which rules are they breaking? Complete the sentences.

1 Students can't bring _____ to school.

2 Students' shoes must be _____ .

3 Girls can't wear short _____ .

4 Boys must wear a _____ with their trousers.

5 No students are allowed to wear _____ .

6 Boys aren't allowed to have _____ hair.

c What do you think of the rules at Martin's school? Prepare to give your opinion in the next class.

④ Vocabulary

Memory

a Put the boxes in order. Write the words in the correct list.

emin	y rem	rise	~~forg~~
r mi	d me	nd m	et r
embe	emo	mor	

Verbs

~~forget~~

r...

....

....

Nouns

....

....

b There is a mistake in each of these sentences. ~~Cross out~~ the wrong word(s) and write the correct word(s).

1 Keep repeating these rules until you memories them. ....

2 I must remember Clare to buy some milk on her way home. ....

3 He's got a very good mind, so I don't think he'll forget my phone number. ....

4 I love this song and I've learnt all the words with my heart. ....

5 Don't forget bringing your camera with you tomorrow. ....

6 Why did she say that? I don't understand how her remind works! ....

⑤ Grammar Grammar reference: page 90

Passive review

a Match the two parts of the sentences.

1 The bridge was ☐
2 French is ☐
3 The decision will be ☐
4 Olive oil has been ☐
5 These songs weren't ☐
6 The lasagne can be ☐

A sung by Elvis Presley.

B reheated in the microwave.

C built in 2004.

D produced in Spain for centuries.

E spoken in many African countries.

F made by the President.

b Choose the correct word and complete the sentences with the past participle form of the verbs.

record	repair	write	give
play	build	make	

1 Both albums *are / were* ....at the Interscope studios in 2010.

2 Table tennis *isn't / wasn't* usually ....outdoors.

3 When *was / has* this book ....?

4 Lots of new houses *have / are* been ....here recently.

5 The boxes *are / been* .... of very strong cardboard.

6 A prize will *be / been* .... to the winner of the competition.

7 Sorry, these speakers *can't / don't* be .... You'll have to get some new ones.

> **Check it out!**
>
> **Don't forget to check for irregular past participles.**

c Complete the questions and give true answers. Write full sentences for your answers.

1 When ....your favourite actor born?

....
....

2 Where ....good clothes sold in your town?

....
....

3 Where ....your computer made?

....
....

4 ....your favourite programme been shown on TV this week? If so, when?

....
....

d Rewrite the underlined words in the passive form.

[1]A fire damaged the museum last week and [2]people can't use the building at the moment. Builders are repairing it now and [3]they will finish the work before the end of the month.

1 ....

2 ....

3 ....

Milton Vale is getting ready for next month's jazz festival. [4]They hold this popular festival every year and [5]they have already sold over 3,000 tickets. [6]You can find information on the festival website.

4 ....

5 ....

6 ....

Help yourself!

Question tags with passives

Remember, to add a question tag to a statement:

- use the auxiliary or modal verb from the statement
- change it from positive to negative or from negative to positive
- use the correct pronoun.

Look at these examples with active statements.

Emily **doesn't** *speak German,* **does** *she?*

The boys **were** *arguing,* **weren't** *they?*

Your phone **can** *download music,* **can't** *it?*

Now try to complete these examples, which are passive statements.

1 This bag was made in Argentina, wasn't it ?

2 Japanese isn't taught in your school, ...?

3 The vegetables weren't cooked properly, ...?

4 Diego's motorbike hasn't been repaired yet, ...?

5 These trousers can be washed in warm water, ...?

6 Your project won't be finished by tomorrow, ...?

6 Pronunciation

Final *e*

a 🔊 **30** Listen and tick (✓) the words you hear. Then listen again and repeat.

1	bit	☐	bite	☐
2	hat	☐	hate	☐
3	hop	☐	hope	☐
4	plan	☐	plane	☐
5	hid	☐	hide	☐
6	cut	☐	cute	☐
7	rod	☐	rode	☐

b 🔊 **31** Look at the phonetic symbols and write the words. Then listen and repeat.

1 /faɪl/ .... 4 /sməʊk/ ....

2 /meɪt/ .... 5 /teɪst/ ....

3 /nəʊt/ .... 6 /waɪd/ ....

c 🔊 **32** Listen and practise saying the sentences.

My mate Sam hates that game.

I hope Tom wrote a note to Olga.

Did the kids arrive in time for dinner?

Practise saying these words

🔊 **33** allowed   competitive   concentrate experiment   importance   memorise punishment   remind   research responsibility   shave   silence

7 Read

a Read the page from a school newsletter. Match these three paragraphs with the activities.

School improvements ☐   Arts Marathon ☐   Winners! ☐

1 competitive events   2 an activity that raised money   3 an activity that will cost money

July Newsletter

🏛 **West Leadbridge School**

This term has been extremely busy – with exams, of course, but also with Year 10 work experience, Science Week, the wonderful production of Shakespeare's *Hamlet* and many other activities. For the first time a ski and snowboarding trip to Austria was organised in February for Year 10 and 11 students, in addition to visits to northern France (Year 9), Madrid (Years 8 and 10) and Rome (Year 12). Many thanks to all the teachers for their hard work in organising these activities.

My very best wishes to you all for the summer and the best of luck to all those students awaiting exam results in August.

Mrs A Short
(Headteacher)

School improvements

Part of the music block has been redesigned as a Music Technology Room, with top-quality ICT equipment to help students with their music composition work. Also, during the holidays, nearly £300,000 will be spent on improving our PE facilities. The old changing rooms and showers in the gym will be replaced and a new dance studio will be added.

Arts Marathon

Early in July we had our annual Arts Marathon – a 12-hour programme of music, art, dance and drama, organised by a student committee with the help of Miss Fry. Over 250 different performances took place, giving students the experience of performing in front of a live audience. The event raised £2,300 for the Red Cross.

Winners!

Congratulations to Alan Firth, who was selected for the Yorkshire Under-18 Rugby Squad. This means he will be busy in September and October competing in the county championships. These games are watched by the England selectors, so it could be the start of a great career for Alan! Another of our students, Tracy Cooper, was awarded first prize in the Under-16 Open Ice Skating Competition in June. This was an excellent result, especially as she has been skating competitively for only one year.

b Find this information:

1 someone who will be doing something exciting in the autumn
....

2 a foreign country that was visited by Year 11 students
....

3 a new facility which has been provided for the school
....

4 a play that was performed during the term
....

5 someone who came top in a sports event
....

6 something that won't be known until next month
....

7 an amount of money that was given to another organisation
....

8 a building which is planned for the school
....

Portfolio 5

Write three paragraphs on different topics for a newsletter from your school. Use the passive when it is suitable.

Here are some possible ideas:

- school facilities
  (e.g. new equipment, changes to buildings, something that was damaged or stolen)
- special events
  (e.g. an exhibition or performance, a school trip, a talk by a visiting speaker, after-school activities)
- sports
- individual achievements
  (e.g. someone who was given a prize or has done something unusual).

Quiz ⑤

a What do you remember about Unit 5? Answer all the questions you can and then check in the Student's Book.

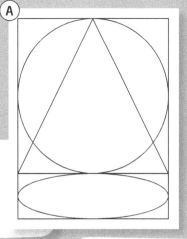

Ⓐ

Ⓑ

1 In picture A there are:

.... triangle(s) .... oval(s)

.... square(s) .... rectangle(s)

.... circle(s)

2 Complete the sentences.

Lisa came top .... all her subjects, but she's .... detention this afternoon because she skived .... after lunch yesterday.

3 Ⓒircle the correct words.

If you don't *retake / revise / research* the work that you've been taught, you might *cheat / pass / fail* the exam.

4 There are three mistakes in this dialogue. Write the correct sentences.

A: Do your teachers let you to wear earrings?

B: No, they can't. We don't allow to wear any jewellery.

....

....

5 Who is the boy in picture B?

....

6 Which three letters are needed to complete these words?

ory

re ☐☐☐ ber

orise

7 Make words to complete the sentence.

he for re le   arn get art mind

Please .... your brother to .... his PIN number by .... so he won't .... it.

8 Complete the sentence with passive verbs.

These programmes .... (make) 20 years ago, but they .... often .... (show) on TV today.

9 Rewrite the sentence in the passive form.

They recorded the album last month, but they haven't released it yet.

....

....

10 Ⓒircle the words that contain the sound /aɪ/.

fine   fitted   invite   revise

spider   decision

b 🔊 34 Listen and check your answers.

c Now look at your Student's Book and write three more quiz questions for Unit 5.

Question: ....

....

Answer: ....

Question: ....

....

Answer: ....

Question: ....

....

Answer: ....

6 Who's got talent?

1 Vocabulary

Noun suffixes

a Complete the table by adding suffixes.

Noun, verb or adjective	Noun
1 select	....
2 excite	....
3 real	....
4 appear	....
5 style	....
6 creative	....
7 exhibit	....
8 entertain	....
9 design	....

b 🔊 35 Complete the text with the correct form of the words in brackets. Then listen and check.

Elise Holdgate is a professional [1]...................................... (sing) who first [2].. (appear) in public in a talent show called *Starlight*. The series [3].. (create) a lot of [4].. (excite) and over nine million viewers were watching when Elise and three other [5].. (final) competed for the big prize on the last night. Elise was not [6].. (select) as the winner, but her wonderful [7].. (perform) led to a recording contract in early 2011. She is now one of the country's top-selling recording [8].. (art).

2 Grammar   Grammar reference: page 80

Past perfect

a Complete the sentences with the past perfect form of the verbs.

have	be	study	begin	see	eat
not hear	not land				

1 I .... already .... the film when I bought the DVD.
2 By the time they got to the theatre, the play ....
3 We .... of this comedian until he appeared on *The Late Show*.
4 .... you .... any dance lessons before you joined this class?
5 The plane .... when we got to the airport.
6 Before Alexander got his first film part, he .... on TV a few times.
7 Until we went to the Penang Café, I .... never .... Malaysian food.
8 .... Emily .... music before she started writing songs?

b Make sentences about what had happened earlier. Use the past perfect form of the verbs.

| have | miss | break | burn |
| not ring | not pass | | |

her	the meat	my Science test
an argument with his friend	his train
her glasses		

Everyone was annoyed at dinner time on Friday.

1 My mother ....
2 My father ....
3 Grandma ....
4 I ....
5 Alex ....
6 Sara's boyfriend ....

c There is a mistake in each of these sentences. ~~Cross out~~ the wrong word(s) and write the correct word(s).

1 We just had finished lunch when Sandro arrived.

....

2 Had you ever spoke to Paula before she contacted you?

....

3 When they went to Japan, they didn't fly in a plane before.

....

4 When I got to the park, all my friends left already.

....

5 Before Josef had come top in the poetry competition, he'd never won a prize.

....

6 How long were they in Madrid when you met them?

....

3 Vocabulary

Entertainment collocations

a Complete the entertainment collocations and write the words in the puzzle. Then use the ◯ letters to make one more collocation.

1 an ....museum
2 ....attention
3 a ....designer
4 a studio ....
5 prize ....
6 ....TV
7 ....talent
8 a ....champion
9 a sports ....

b Complete the sentences with collocations from Exercise 3a.

1 Harry has shown amazing skill with the football since he was five years old. He's got a ....for the game.

2 She became a .... in judo when she won her gold medal in the 2008 Olympics.

3 We were in the .... when they recorded the comedy show, and we watched it again when it was shown on TV last night.

4 He's a top .... in Milan. The clothes he creates are amazing, but they're also very expensive to buy.

5 Whatever they do, film stars are followed by photographers and journalists. It's often hard to cope with all this ....

6 There's a great collection of Impressionist paintings at the ....in Peel Street.

c Think of an example for each of the following.

1 a popular fashion designer
....

2 a TV programme which is recorded in front of a studio audience
....

3 someone who has had a lot of media attention recently
....

4 a sports star who earns lots of money
....

5 a reality TV show that you enjoy
....

6 someone from your country who is or was a world champion
....

(4) Listen

a 📢 36 Listen to the conversations (1–3) about TV shows and match them with the pictures. There is one extra picture.

b 📢 36 Listen again. Are the sentences *right* (✓) or *wrong* (✗)?

Show 1

1 Martina isn't going to audition for the show. ☐

2 More than 30 million people watch the show each week. ☐

3 The prize is a contract with a record company. ☐

Show 2

4 The woman on TV isn't a professional performer. ☐

5 When the man first appeared on the show, he hadn't trained as a dancer before. ☐

6 There are four judges on the show. ☐

Show 3

7 At the beginning of the series, there are 24 people in the competition. ☐

8 The show is always recorded in a restaurant. ☐

9 The competition lasts for about two months. ☐

5 Grammar Grammar reference: page 80

Past perfect continuous

a Complete the sentences with the past perfect continuous form of the verbs.

1 I met Janet on my way home. She _____ _____ (study) in the library.

2 It was sad when we had to cut down the tree outside my window. It _____ _____ (grow) there for 15 years.

3 Luke was amazed when he came top in the exam. He _____ (not expect) it.

4 **A:** My aunt left the company in 2008.
   B: How long _____ (she / work) there?

5 Rosa had a terrible argument with Giorgio on Friday. And they _____ (get on) so well together before that!

6 We _____ (not walk) for long when the rain started to come down.

b Complete the sentences so that the meaning is the same. Use the past perfect continuous and the word in brackets.

1 They worked all afternoon. In the evening they were tired.
   (because)
   They were tired in the evening _____
   _____ .

2 People were living here for centuries. Then in 1850 the volcano erupted.
   (before)
   _____
   _____ the volcano erupted in 1850.

3 Steve wanted to enter the dance competition, but then he broke his arm.
   (hoping)
   Before Steve broke his arm, _____
   _____ .

4 At 7 o'clock I arrived at the cinema. Twenty minutes later Danielle arrived.
   (waiting)
   When Danielle arrived at the cinema, _____
   _____ .

c Circle the correct words.

Ben's face was bright red. He had ¹*sat / been sitting* outside in the sun and he had ²*fallen / been falling* asleep. He hadn't ³*put on / been putting on* any sun cream, so his skin was burnt.

Mia was hungry when she got home because she had ⁴*played / been playing* in the band for almost four hours and they hadn't ⁵*stopped / been stopping* for lunch. They had ⁶*practised / been practising* for the school talent show.

6 Pronunciation

Changing word stress

a 🔊 37 Listen and <u>underline</u> the stressed syllable in these words. Then listen again and repeat.

1 piano   pianist
2 compete   competition
3 flexible   flexibility
4 communicate   communication
5 advertise   advertisement
6 impossible   impossibility

b 🔊 38 Tick (✓) the word pair if you think the stress is different. Then listen, check and <u>underline</u> the stressed syllable in each word.

1 perform   performance   ☐
2 celebrate   celebration   ☐
3 electric   electricity   ☐
4 agree   agreement   ☐
5 travel   traveller   ☐
6 national   nationality   ☐

Practise saying these words

🔊 39 audition   creativity   disappointment
education   entertainment   excitement
journalist   judge   photographer
selection   talented

(7) Read

a Read the article about Justin Bieber and choose the best title for it.

A The amazing success of Justin Bieber

B Justin Bieber's early life

C A biography of Justin Bieber

ON 9 NOVEMBER 2010 Justin Bieber reached the 1 billion mark for views of his videos on YouTube, just a few weeks after Lady Gaga had become the first to hit this total. The video for his hit song *Baby* had already scored a record-breaking 370 million views earlier in the year. He had 12 million fans on Facebook and 5.5 million people were following his news on Twitter. And he was just 16 years old.

Three-and-a-half years earlier, Justin had been living as an ordinary 13-year-old kid in a Canadian town. When he entered a talent show in March 2007, his mother put some videos of his performances on YouTube for his friends and family to see. From here, his rise to fame began. Justin had already attracted plenty of fans when music manager Scooter Braun clicked onto one of his videos and liked what he saw. In partnership with the rap artist Usher,

Braun arranged for a contract with Island Records in October 2008. A year later, Justin's first album *My World* came out and sold millions around the world.

By the end of 2010 Justin had made many appearances on TV, he had toured the US and Canada and he was working on a film. He had performed with some of America's top musicians and sung for the US President. He had released a range of perfumes. He had even written his own autobiography! None of this would have been possible 20 years ago, before the global popularity of 'social media' like YouTube, Facebook and Twitter. You may love Justin Bieber or hate him, but you must agree that he certainly knows how to use the amazing power of the web to his advantage.

b Choose the correct answer: A, B or C.

1 Lady Gaga got 1 billion video views

   A in October 2010.

   B a short time after Justin Bieber.

   C a long time before Justin Bieber.

2 Justin Bieber set a record for his song *Baby*

   A in November 2010.

   B before November 2010.

   C after November 2010.

3 In March 2007 Justin

   A was thirteen years old.

   B had moved from his home in Canada.

   C had already met Scooter Braun.

4 Justin became world-famous

   A when he appeared in a talent show.

   B with the help of his family and friends.

   C because of a video on YouTube.

5 When *My World* was released,

   A not many people knew about Justin.

   B Justin had already got a lot of fans.

   C Justin started to get fans.

6 By December 2010 Justin

   A had been planning a tour of North America.

   B had made a movie.

   C had given a performance for the President.

7 He wrote a book

   A when he was twenty.

   B about the social media.

   C about his own life.

c What do you think of Justin Bieber? Do you think he deserved his fame when he was 16? Prepare to talk about this in your next lesson.

Portfolio 6

Describe someone who has become a celebrity through the social media or in a TV show.

- When and how did he/she become so popular?
- What had he/she been doing before that?
- What is your opinion of him/her?

Quiz 6

a What do you remember about Unit 6? Answer all the questions you can and then check in the Student's Book.

A

1 Which TV talent show was won by the young woman in picture A?

....

2 Match the words with their suffixes to make nouns.

1	select	A	-ment
2	style	B	-ity
3	entertain	C	-ion
4	real	D	-ist

3 Complete the sentence with the correct nouns.

creative   exhibit   art

The .... is great. You'll be amazed by the ....'s

....

4 (Circle) the nouns with the stress on the <u>second</u> syllable.

possibility   comedian   reality
finalist   photographer

5 Write the question and answer. Use the past perfect.

A: That comedian was funny on Sunday.
B: you / ever / see / him before?

....

A: No, I / never / hear / of him.

....

B

1			M				
		2	E				
3			D				
4			I				
5			A				

6 Put the words in order and write the sentence.

an audience / sung / the competition / before she / hadn't / She / in front of / entered

....

....

7 When Mozart wrote his first symphony, how long had he been learning music?

....

8 Complete the sentence. Use the past perfect and past perfect continuous.

Tom .... (not get) home when I called because he .... (work) late.

9 Use the words in the box to make three entertainment collocations. There are two extra words.

museum   natural   star   entertainment
talent   art   musician   sports

....

....

10 Complete the puzzle in picture B with words from these collocations.

1 world ....   2 fashion ....   3 studio ....
4 .... money   5 .... TV

b 🔊 40 Listen and check your answers.

c Now look at your Student's Book and write three more quiz questions for Unit 6.

Question: ....

....

Answer: ....

Question: ....

....

Answer: ....

Question: ....

....

Answer: ....

7 That's incredible!

1 Vocabulary

Extreme adjectives

a Make nine extreme adjectives. Use one letter from each column.

		¹E	X	H	A	U	S	T	E	D				
2									3					
		4				5								
6						7								
		8												
	9													

```
            W   F   L   G       H       G
            E   Z   I   Y   L   T   O   B
        A   B   H   U   I   S   I   U   D   L
        U   R   X   E   A   R   E   V   E   I   E   N
    F   E   R   E   I   T   N   I   V   G   A   G   L   I   Y
    T   R   E   N   S   F   A   U   N   B   N   T   I   E   N   G
```

b 🔊 41 Complete the sentences with extreme adjectives. Then listen and check.

A: Was it exciting? Did you enjoy it?
B: No, it was ¹ .... (bad)! I know lots of people love doing it, but to me it was absolutely ² .... (frightening).

We hadn't been able to see much because of the fog, but around midday it cleared away and we got a view of these ³ .... (big) mountains for the first time. It was ⁴ .... (surprising).

It was ⁵ .... (hot) out on the court and they played for four hours. By the end of the match they were both ⁶ .... (tired).

We were caught in a snow storm which lasted all day. So it was ⁷ .... (cold) outside and we had to stay inside this ⁸ .... (small) tent. And of course we couldn't cook any food to eat, so we were ⁹ .... (hungry)!

2 Grammar

Grammar reference: page 92

Modal verbs of deduction: present

a Match the two parts of the sentences.

1 This creature hasn't got eight legs, so it ☐
2 Don't climb on that wall. It ☐
3 Anna isn't at school today. She ☐
4 I can see smoke in the distance. It ☐
5 There are no plates in the cupboard. They ☐
6 It's windy outside, but it ☐

A could be a forest fire.
B might not be cold.
C can't be a spider.
D may be ill.
E might be dangerous.
F must be in the dishwasher.

b Complete the dialogues with modal verbs. Sometimes there is more than one possible answer.

1 A: I haven't had anything to eat today.
   B: Really? You .... be starving!

2 A: Can you remember Ahmed's phone number?
   B: No, but you could try asking Pete. He .... know it.

3 A: Have we got any orange juice?
   B: I'm not sure. There .... be some in the fridge.

4 A: I think the story of Dracula is true.
   B: Oh no, you .... believe that! It's just an old legend.

5 A: I'm thinking of making an Indian dish on Saturday. Does that sound OK?
   B: It's fine with me, but I'm not sure about Laura. She .... like Indian food.

c Make three deductions with modal verbs about the animal in the photo. Use your own ideas.

It must be a wild animal.

1 ....
....

2 ....
....

3 ....
....

3 Vocabulary

Phrasal verbs with *go*

a Match the underlined verbs with their meanings.

| chased | continued | returned |
| revised | toured | left |

1 The party <u>went on</u> until one o'clock in the morning.
....

2 I <u>went over</u> my notes carefully before I started writing my essay.
....

3 They said goodbye to the woman and she <u>went away</u>.
....

4 She realised she had left her umbrella in the café, so she <u>went back</u> to get it.
....

5 We <u>went round</u> the castle with a guide from the tourist office.
....

6 The cat ran across the garden and our dog <u>went after</u> it.
....

b Choose the right answer: A, B or C.

A: I went round to the old Henderson house yesterday to look for a tennis ball that had gone into the garden. You know Mrs Henderson went [1]......... a few years ago, so the house is empty now.

B: Yes, that's right.

A: Well, it was weird. I know nobody was there, but I seemed to hear the sound of someone laughing inside the house. It went [2]......... for three or four minutes and then it suddenly stopped.

B: What was going [3].........?

A: I don't know, but I'm not going to go [4]......... to find out. It was a frightening experience and I don't want to go [5]......... it again.

1 **A** out   **B** back   **C** away
2 **A** on   **B** out   **C** through
3 **A** on   **B** over   **C** about
4 **A** away   **B** after   **C** back
5 **A** over   **B** through   **C** round

Help yourself!

Practice with phrasal verbs

These sentences contain phrasal verbs that you have seen in Units 1–6. Complete them with the words in the box.

on	off	down	up	to	away
across	through				

1 You'll need to explain the idea clearly to get your meaning .... to everyone.

2 The concert is on next week. I'm really looking forward .... it.

3 We always warm .... with some stretching exercises before the match.

4 Some people don't like Teresa much, but I get .... well with her.

5 I'm so tired. I don't think I can get .... this football match.

6 When the vegetables have cooled .... , put them into the food processor.

7 Many villages were cut .... for days because of the flood. No one could get in or out.

8 You'll have to throw that meat .... It's been in the fridge for ages.

Remember to keep a list of phrasal verbs with example sentences, and revise them often.

(4) Grammar Grammar reference: page 92

Modal verbs of deduction: past

a Complete the sentences with the correct form of the verbs.

be	like	break	go out	buy	oversleep
forget	disappear				

1 You should ask a doctor to look at your finger. I think you might .... it.

2 Karl missed the bus this morning. He must ....

3 My sunglasses must be in the house somewhere. They can't .... !

4 They didn't spend much time at the shopping mall, so they might not .... anything.

5 I didn't get a call from Jane last night. Could she .... to ring me?

6 Everyone was talking about Evan's party. It must .... a big success.

7 They may .... I can't see their car anywhere.

8 I'm not sure why Tim left the concert early. He may not .... the music.

b Rewrite the sentences using modal verbs.

1 Perhaps you dropped your wallet in the car park.

....
....

2 I'm sure Danny went round to Adam's place.

....
....

3 Maybe your friend didn't write this email.

....
....

4 It's possible that Rachel borrowed some money from her sister.

....
....

5 I'm certain that the book didn't fall out of my bag.

....
....

6 I'm worried because I'm not sure I passed the exam.

....
....

c Look at the picture. What could have happened? Use your own ideas and write four sentences.

1 (must) The driver ....
....

2 (may) ....
....

3 (might) ....
....

4 (could) ....
....

5 Read

a Read the text and comments from a website about Dover Castle. Tick (✓) the three people who had similar experiences in the underground tunnels.

http://interactive.cambridge.org

Dover Castle

Dover Castle on the south coast of England is a popular tourist attraction. As well as exploring the 12th- and 13th-century buildings, visitors can take a tour of the amazing tunnels under the castle. These tunnels were made in the 18th century and during World War II they became a centre of secret war-time operations, with underground offices, telephone and radio rooms and a hospital. Many visitors say they have seen the ghosts of people who lived and worked here during that time.

Comments

Angie ☐

I visited the castle in 2009. The guide was taking my group along one of the tunnels when I looked back behind me and I saw a man in uniform. He was holding something, maybe papers. He walked across the corridor and then disappeared into the wall! It was amazing. No one else in the group noticed anything, but I definitely saw this.

Phil ☐

Last July my friend and I were at the front of our group near the hospital. When we turned a corner we both saw a man walking across the tunnel and he went through a metal door. He was dressed in army uniform. At first we thought it was probably an actor in a costume, but when we got to the door, we found that it was locked and couldn't be opened. We didn't say anything because we didn't think anyone would believe us. It wasn't an awful experience, but it was very strange.

Simon ☐

Phil, I've seen the same man twice near the hospital. I think it might be a film projected onto the wall by the tour organisers, to make the tour more interesting. However, I couldn't see any camera equipment anywhere and I'm keeping an open mind.

Debbie ☐

I haven't actually seen a ghost, but there's an area near one of the stairways that I find terrifying. It always feels freezing and it makes the hairs stand up on the back of my neck. One time when I was walking there I felt someone push me quite hard from behind. When I turned round there was nobody there. I was glad to get away from there.

b Look at the comments and complete the sentences with the names: Angie, Phil, Simon or Debbie.

1 .... has never seen anything unusual in the underground tunnels.

2 .... thought the man he/she saw might have been an actor.

3 .... saw a person holding something in his hand.

4 .... has felt frightened when visiting the castle.

5 .... believes there may be a normal explanation for what he/she saw.

6 .... was the only person in his/her group who saw something unusual.

7 .... and .... have visited Dover Castle more than once.

6 Pronunciation

Elision of *have*

a 🔊 42 Listen to the pronunciation of *have*. Tick (✓) *weak* if the vowel sound is /ə/ or *strong* if it is /æ/. Then listen again and repeat.

	weak	strong
1 I always **have** a shower in the morning.	☐	☐
2 Where **have** you put my shirt?	☐	☐
3 I might **have** put it in the washing machine.	☐	☐
4 They must **have** gone to the cinema.	☐	☐
5 You haven't made your bed, **have** you?	☐	☐
6 Yes, I **have**.	☐	☐
7 **Have** they heard this song before?	☐	☐
8 Yes, they **have**.	☐	☐

b 🔊 **43** Listen and practise saying these sentences.

I'll have lunch after I've been to the bank.

Have they been shopping or have they been to the cinema?

My parents have been having problems with the car.

7 Listen

a 🔊 **45** Listen to Part 1 of the recording and write the information.

City: Salamanca

Country: ¹ ....

Church: built in the ² .... century

Clothes and equipment in the sculpture: space suit, ³ ...., backpack, ⁴ ....

First astronaut: ⁵19..............

b 🔊 **46** Listen to Part 2. Complete the three explanations for the astronaut at Salamanca. Which do you think is the most likely?

1   Someone must have created the photo using a ....

2   People might have been able to see or travel into the ....

3   The builders must have seen .... from ....

c 🔊 **47** Listen to Part 3. What is the real explanation?

....

Portfolio 7

Read this post on a discussion board and write a reply. Talk about your own experiences, or things you have heard or read about, and give your opinions. Use some modals of deduction in your answer.

I think it's strange that so many people still don't believe that aliens from other planets exist. People all over the world have reported seeing strange lights and metal objects in the sky, and if you look on the internet, you can find lots of photos of these things. Some people say they have actually had contact with aliens or been inside alien spaceships. I personally haven't had any experience like this, but I believe there must be some truth in these stories. What do other people think?

Quiz 7

a What do you remember about Unit 7? Answer all the questions you can and then check in the Student's Book.

A

B

1 Match the adjectives.
- **1** hot ☐
- **2** big ☐
- **3** small ☐
- **A** huge
- **B** tiny
- **C** boiling

2 Which adjective is the odd one out?
weird strange surprised
mysterious unbelievable

3 Circle the correct words.
A: Are you hungry?
B: Yes, I'm *very / absolutely* *starving / freezing* !

4 What does this sentence mean? Tick (✓) the correct sentences.
I'm certain it's an expensive camera.
- **A** It must be expensive. ☐
- **B** It may cost a lot of money. ☐
- **C** It might not cost much. ☐
- **D** It can't be cheap. ☐

5 What is the name of the boy in picture A?
....

6 How long have the crocodile and the man in picture B been friends?
....

7 Replace the underlined words with phrasal verbs with *go*.
I ¹continued working for half an hour and then I ²left the house.
1 .... 2 ....

8 Complete the phrasal verbs. Choose words from the box.

after about out on round

I heard loud music outside so I went .... and I saw that a party was going .... in the street.

9 Circle the correct words.
Danny was able to walk home after the accident, so he *can't / mustn't* have *broke / broken* his leg.

10 There are mistakes in this sentence. Write the correct sentence.
Sally might not speak to David yesterday, but she must have saw him.
....
....

b 🔊48 Listen and check your answers.

c Now look at your Student's Book and write three more quiz questions for Unit 7.

Question: ....
....
Answer: ....

Question: ....
....
Answer: ....

Question: ....
....
Answer: ....

8 Gaming and gadgets

1 Vocabulary

Health problems

a Complete the crossword.

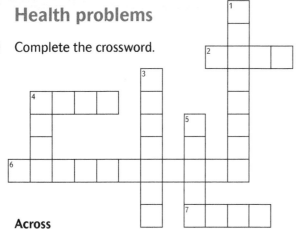

Across

2 I've got a .... in my shoulder.

4 I feel ....

6 I've got a ....

7 My feet ....

Down

1 I've got a ....

3 I've got a .... ache.

4 I've got a .... leg.

5 I've got a ....

b There is a mistake in each of these sentences. ~~Cross out~~ the wrong word(s) and write the correct word(s).

1 He won't want to sing if he's got a hurt throat.

....

2 Have you got headache?

....

3 Some people feel dizy when they look down from a tall building.

....

4 She should stay at home if she's got cold.

....

5 You've got the temperature.

....

6 I've cut my finger and it really pains!

....

7 Andy has to stay in bed because he's got a flue.

....

2 Grammar Grammar reference: page 94

Quantifiers review

a Match the two parts of the sentences.

1 There's too much ☐

2 That table is too ☐

3 I'm not strong enough ☐

4 You've put too many ☐

5 There have been fewer ☐

6 Have we made enough ☐

7 Video games take less ☐

A storms this autumn than usual.

B clothes in the washing machine.

C big to fit in my room.

D sandwiches for everyone?

E pepper in the sauce.

F time to load than they used to.

G to carry this on my own.

> **Check it out!**
>
> With adjectives, make sure you can see the difference between *very* and *too*. *Very* adds extra strength to the adjective, but *too* means 'more than what is wanted or needed'.

b Complete the sentences with *a few*, *fewer* or *less*.

1 .... tracks on this album are OK, but most of them are disappointing.

2 You should eat more fruit and .... junk food.

3 This year there were .... people at the festival than last year.

4 Our dog is getting old. He has .... energy than he used to have.

5 I always look at .... different websites when I'm searching for information.

6 You'll have .... problems with your computer if you increase the memory.

c Complete the sentences with *enough*, *too*, *too much* or *too many* and the words in the box.

food   time   people   calls   noise   warm   late   busy

1 It's already nearly midnight. It's .... to start watching the film now.

2 It's impossible to concentrate! There's .... outside.

3 I didn't have .... to finish the Geography exam.

4 Don't make .... on my phone. They're expensive!

5 Clare can't meet us for lunch today. She's .... at work.

6 The room was so crowded that no one could dance. They'd invited ....

7 It wasn't .... to go swimming yesterday.

8 You've given me .... I'm afraid I can't eat it all.

d 🔊 **49** Choose the correct answer: A, B or C. Then listen and check.

A: Oh, I'm feeling a bit sick.

B: Maybe you ate ¹.......... chocolates. Come and sit down for ².......... minutes.

A: No, I think I'll go outside. It's ³.......... hot in here and there ⁴.......... fresh air.

1	**A** many	**B** too many	**C** too much
2	**A** few	**B** fewer	**C** a few
3	**A** too	**B** too much	**C** enough
4	**A** 's enough	**B** isn't enough	**C** 's too much

A: Are you OK, Mike?

B: Yeah, not bad, but I've been having ⁵.......... headaches lately.

A: I don't think you're getting ⁶.......... exercise. Can't you spend ⁷.......... time in front of the computer? Why don't you take a break now?

B: No, not right now – there's ⁸.......... work that I have to finish. After this weekend it'll be better. I'll have ⁹.......... things to do then.

5	**A** a few	**B** fewer	**C** less
6	**A** enough	**B** less	**C** too much
7	**A** much	**B** fewer	**C** less
8	**A** too many	**B** too much	**C** not enough
9	**A** enough	**B** less	**C** fewer

③ Vocabulary

Technology

a Circle the correct words in these computer expressions.

1 a voice-*connected* / *activated* / *attached* device

2 run *through* / *over* / *out of* battery

3 plug *in* / *on* / *up* a machine

4 a *feel* / *touch* / *hold* screen

5 a games *file* / *keyboard* / *console*

6 a memory *button* / *card* / *cable*

b Complete the sentences.

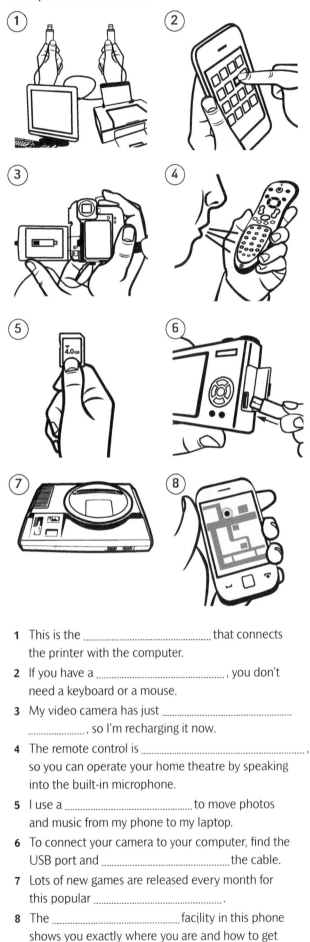

1 This is the .... that connects the printer with the computer.

2 If you have a .... , you don't need a keyboard or a mouse.

3 My video camera has just .... , so I'm recharging it now.

4 The remote control is .... , so you can operate your home theatre by speaking into the built-in microphone.

5 I use a .... to move photos and music from my phone to my laptop.

6 To connect your camera to your computer, find the USB port and .... the cable.

7 Lots of new games are released every month for this popular ....

8 The .... facility in this phone shows you exactly where you are and how to get to your destination.

(4) Pronunciation

Words with *gh*

a 🔊 **50** Tick (✓) the words which end in the sound /f/. Then listen, check and repeat.

cough	☐	laugh	☐
tough	☐	weigh	☐
through	☐	enough	☐
although	☐	high	☐

b 🔊 **51** Which vowel sound do you hear? Write the words in the correct list. Then listen, check and repeat.

~~light~~   ~~bought~~   ~~tough~~   ~~weigh~~
thought   eight   right   brought   flight
rough   straight   n<u>eigh</u>bour   en<u>ough</u>
fr<u>igh</u>tened   d<u>augh</u>ter

/ʌ/	/aɪ/
tough....................	light....................
....	....
....	....

/ɔː/	/eɪ/
bought....................	weigh....................
....	....
....	....

c 🔊 **52** Listen and practise saying these sentences.

I thought she was coughing, but she was laughing.

We went through a tough time during the drought.

Our neighbour's daughter hasn't brought enough money.

Practise saying these words

🔊 **53** admire   annoying   cable console   crowded   headache investigation   launch   politician portable   require   stomach ache

---

⑤ Read

a Read the text and match the paragraphs (1–4) with the topics (A–E). There is one extra topic.

A Asimo's appearance ☐   **C** General information about Asimo ☐   **E** Asimo's skills ☐

B The history of robots ☐   **D** Future use of this technology ☐

Asimo

❶ In October 2010 the Honda company celebrated the tenth birthday of Asimo, their multi-talented humanoid robot. Since his creation in 2000, Asimo has been constantly updated to show new skills, and he is probably the world's most impressive product of robot technology.

❷ Getting a robot to stand and move about easily on two legs is extremely difficult, but Asimo now moves like a real human being. He can walk, turn, balance on one foot and go up and down stairs. He can run at 6km per hour and can avoid moving objects while he is running. The cameras which are his 'eyes' can recognise faces and objects, and he can follow spoken instructions.

❸ With a height of 1.2m and weighing 43kg, Asimo is big enough to do useful jobs but small enough to seem friendly. In fact he looks rather like a child in a space suit. While his movements copy those of a real person, his face is less life-like, with fewer human features, than some other robots. This is because research has shown that when robots start to look too much like living humans, people find them 'creepy' and feel less comfortable with them.

❹ The company expects that Asimo robots will soon be used to help people in their homes, especially people who are elderly or too ill to do a lot for themselves. For example, the robot will be able to bring their medicine, turn on lights, answer the door, serve food and drink and provide communication through the internet. Later versions of Asimo might be able to do jobs that are dangerous for humans, like fire fighting or working in unhealthy conditions. 'We want people to understand that robots are not what they have seen on TV or in movies like *The Terminator*,' says Honda project leader Stephen Keeney. 'These are machines that will really make our lives better in the future.'

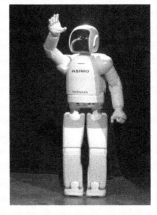

b Are the sentences *right* (✓), *wrong* (✗) or *doesn't say* (–)?

1 Asimo is now over ten years old. ☐

2 The Honda company first started making robots in 2000. ☐

3 It is too difficult to make a robot move like a person. ☐

4 Asimo is voice-activated. ☐

5 Most humanoid robots are taller than Asimo. ☐

6 People feel uncomfortable with robots which aren't realistic enough. ☐

7 Asimo robots are used by people who can't move around much. ☐

8 In the future they may work in conditions that aren't safe enough for us. ☐

c How would you feel about having one of these robots in your home? How would you use it? Prepare to talk about this in your next class.

⑥ Grammar   Grammar reference: page 94

Non-defining relative clauses

a Complete the sentences with the correct pronoun: *who*, *whose*, *which* or *where*.

1 I'm looking forward to trying this action game, ... came free with the console.

2 Alfred Hitchcock, ... made more than 50 films, was a British director.

3 That shop in Harris Street, ... I used to buy all my clothes, closed down last month.

4 The police spoke to Mr Wingfield, ... house is opposite the school.

5 At the party I met a girl called Petra, ... brother was in my class last year.

6 I found this recipe, ... is very easy to make, on an American website.

b Join the sentences by changing the second sentence to a relative clause.

1 My mother couldn't find anything she wanted on the menu. She doesn't eat meat.

....

....

2 The MLC Building is on the corner of Turner Street. Debra goes there for dance classes.

....

....

3 Adnan and Maya both grew up in Sydney. Their parents come from Malaysia.

....

....

4 This console has multimedia facilities. These are convenient and easy to use.

....

....

5 Carla Davis is a year younger than me. Her painting won the school art prize.

....

....

6 They decided to spend a few days in Stratford. Shakespeare was born there.

....

....

7 Listen

a 🔊 **54** Listen to five people talking about new products. Match the speakers (1–5) with the products in the pictures. There is one extra picture.

Ⓐ 　Ⓑ 　Ⓒ 　Ⓓ 　Ⓔ 　Ⓕ

Kung Fu Showdown

b 🔊 **54** Listen again and complete the table with notes about the products.

	Positive features	Negative features
1		
2		
3		
4		
5		

Portfolio 8

Write a review of a piece of technology that you have bought or used recently. It could be hardware (e.g. a printer, a screen, etc.), software (a computer program or game) or a gadget.

Paragraph 1
• Name and price
• What it is and how it works

Paragraph 2
• How often you use it
• Why you like / don't like it

Paragraph 3
Conclusion: is it good value? Do you recommend it or not?

Quiz 8

a What do you remember about Unit 8? Answer all the questions you can and then check in the Student's Book.

(A)

(B)

1 What is the problem in picture A?

He ....

2 (Circle) the correct words.

I think I've got a *cold / flu*. I've got a *sore / sick* throat and a *pain / cough*.

3 There are mistakes in this sentence. Write the correct sentence.

There's too many sugar in this coffee and there isn't milk enough.

....

....

4 What is the boy doing in picture B?

....

5 Add vowels (*a, e, i, o, u*) and match the words to make three computer nouns.

1 mmry	A scrn
2 gms	B crd
3 tch	C cnsl

....

....

....

6 ~~Cross out~~ the ending which is not correct.

If your phone runs out of battery
A it stops working.
B you can go online.
C you have to recharge it.

7 What does GPS stand for?

....

8 Write the correct pronouns.

Maria, ... mother comes from Greece, is planning a trip to Athens, ... she will stay with her aunt and uncle.

9 Join the sentences.

Alex bought his phone from the shop in Gold Street. It is voice-activated.

....

....

10 Think about the pronunciation. Which is the odd one out?

rough   tough   through   enough

b 🔊 55 Listen and check your answers.

c Now look at your Student's Book and write three more quiz questions for Unit 8.

Question: ....

....

Answer: ....

Question: ....

....

Answer: ....

Question: ....

....

Answer: ....

1 Vocabulary

Adjectives of opinion

a Look at the table: 1 is G, 2 is O and 10 is N. Write all these letters in the puzzle. Then complete the adjectives and write the letters in the table.

1	2	3	4	5	6	7	8	9	10
G	O								N

11	12	13	14	15	16	17	18	19

b Complete the table of opposites. Use adjectives from Exercise 1a.

Adjective	Opposite meaning
1	very beautiful
2	clear, easy to understand
3	extremely ugly
4	unsurprising
5	very boring
6	serious, not funny
7	making you feel calm and relaxed
8	making you feel happy and excited

c (Circle) the correct adjectives.

1 A: Wow! That's a really *impressive / depressing* painting.

    B: Yes, I agree. It's wonderful.

2 A: What did you think of the musical?

    B: It was good. It's got an *amusing / upsetting* story and the costumes are *hideous / gorgeous*.

3 A: This soap opera is *confusing / hideous*. Who's that woman and why is she doing that?

    B: I don't know. There are so many characters! You're never really sure what's happening. It's *shocking / annoying*.

4 A: I failed my Maths exam. It's so *fascinating / depressing*! I really studied hard for it.

    B: Oh, that's *upset / upsetting*. I'm sorry to hear that.

Check it out!

The -ed form of these adjectives describes how we feel.
I was annoyed/confused, etc.

The -ing form describes the thing/ person that produces the feeling.
The mosquitoes were annoying.
This article is confusing!

(2) Grammar Grammar reference: page 96

as if, as though and *like*

a Read the sentence and then decide if the statement below is *right* (✓) or *wrong* (✗).

1 *The bag looks as if it's made of leather.*
It's a leather bag. ☐

2 *It seemed as though he was unhappy.*
I got the feeling he was unhappy. ☐

3 *She looks like her mother.*
They have a similar appearance. ☐

4 *What do you think of music like this?*
Do you like this piece of music? ☐

5 *Windsurfing is a bit like sailing.*
The two sports are quite similar. ☐

b Tick (✓) the correct sentences. If there is a mistake, ~~cross out~~ the wrong word(s) and write the correct word(s).

1 Tim's stories are excellent. He's as if a professional journalist. ....

2 What's wrong with Ann? She looks as though she's been crying. ....

3 Hey, this sculpture's amazing! It's like there's a real person sitting there! ....

4 Visiting the old house was like to go into a museum. ....

5 Can you hear that noise? It looks like an aeroplane. ....

6 It seems as if the image is real, but it's an optical illusion. ....

7 Dolphins, as other mammals, need to breathe air. ....

8 I am afraid I cannot see any talent in these paintings. It is like they were painted by a child. ....

(3) Listen

a 🔊 56 Listen to the dialogues (1–3) and match them with the photos.

b 🔊 56 Listen again and complete the sentences with words from the dialogues.

1 It seems as though the man .... on top of it.

2 They look as if ....

3 When you come here it's like ....

c What are their opinions? For each dialogue, choose the correct answer: A, B or C.

1 The speakers agree that the image is ....
   A beautiful   **B** amusing   **C** confusing

2 One of the speakers thinks the image is ....
   A impressive   **B** depressing   **C** hideous

3 Both speakers think the artwork is ....
   A shocking   **B** impressive   **C** upsetting

d What is your opinion of the three artworks? Prepare to speak about this in your next lesson.

(A)

(B)

(C)

4 Vocabulary

Truth and lies

a Look at the words in bold and write *n* (noun), *v* (verb) or *adj* (adjective).

1 That's a **lie**! It's not true at all. ....

2 He's an honest and **truthful** person. ....

3 Someone has **forged** these documents. ....

4 My brother can do lots of magic **tricks**. ....

5 Believe me! I'm not trying to **fool** you. ....

6 They discovered that the signature was **fake**. ....

7 I hate it when people **lie** to me. ....

8 She was a **fool** to spend so much money on that necklace. ....

b Complete the sentences. Use one word only in each sentence.

1 You can't believe what he says. He often t............................... lies.

2 This is definitely a drawing by Rembrandt. It isn't f............................... .

3 It's very difficult to f............................... money, and it's a serious crime.

4 I said that because I didn't want to hurt his feelings. It was just a little w............................... lie.

5 Please give your honest opinion. I want you to tell the t............................... .

6 The woman seemed to disappear, but of course it was really just a clever t............................... .

7 I know what really happened. You can't t............................... me!

8 He certainly isn't a dishonest person. In fact, he's always very t............................... .

Help yourself!

Idioms: honesty and dishonesty

Do the expressions in **bold** describe honest or dishonest behaviour?
Write *H* or *D*.

1 I believed her story and gave her some money. She really **took me for a ride**. ....

2 I'm not a terrible liar, but I sometimes **bend the truth** a bit. ....

3 Let's **lay our cards on the table**. What do you really think of this situation? ....

4 Do you think he was telling the truth? I'm not sure if he's **on the level**. ....

5 People have confidence in you because you always **play by the rules**. ....

6 Don't trust him. He's **as crooked as a dog's hind leg**. ....

Match the definitions with the expressions in **bold** above.

A to say something that isn't completely true ☐

B to behave honestly ☐

C very dishonest ☐

D to cheat somebody ☐

E honest ☐

F to speak truthfully, without hiding anything ☐

Add these idioms to the list in your notebook.

---

5 Grammar

Grammar reference: page 96

Articles: *a/an*, *the* or no article

a Complete the sentences with *a*, *an* or *the*.

1 Thanks for .... postcard you sent me.

2 I think this is .... brilliant painting.

3 That's .... house where Angela lives.

4 In this photo .... boy on the right is my friend Adam.

5 My mother works in .... office in London.

6 James wants to be .... photographer.

7 I've never seen .... insect like that before!

8 I had a cake and a cup of coffee, but .... cake wasn't very nice.

b 🔊 **57** Complete the text with *a*, *an* or *the*, or leave the space blank where no article is needed. Then listen and check.

Wem is ¹_____ small town in the west of England. In 1995 ²_____ fire started in ³_____ town centre and the town hall was almost completely destroyed. During ⁴_____ fire, ⁵_____ photographer called Tony O'Rahilly took some photos of ⁶_____ burning building. One of these photos was very strange. It showed ⁷_____ young girl standing upstairs with the fire burning all round her.

⁸_____ expert looked at ⁹_____ photo and said it wasn't fake. So was this girl a ghost? Of course, ¹⁰_____ people are fascinated by ¹¹_____

mysteries like this, and Wem became an attraction for visitors who had seen the photo on the internet.

Then in 2010, ¹²_____ elderly man called Brian Lear was looking at ¹³_____ old postcard when he noticed that there was ¹⁴_____ girl standing in the corner of the photo. She looked exactly like ¹⁵_____ girl from the 1995 photo. ¹⁶_____ mystery was solved. Mr O'Rahilly had died five years earlier, but it was clear that his famous photo was a fake after all.

6 Pronunciation
/ð/ and /θ/

a 🔊 **58** Listen and tick (✓) the word you hear. Then listen again and check.

/θ/

1 thick	☐	sick	☐
2 true	☐	threw	☐
3 mouse	☐	mouth	☐
4 three	☐	tree	☐
5 thought	☐	sort	☐

/ð/

6 sat	☐	that	☐
7 then	☐	ten	☐
8 day	☐	they	☐
9 close	☐	clothes	☐
10 although	☐	also	☐

b 🔊 **59** Listen and repeat all the *th* words in Exercise 6a.

c 🔊 **60** Find a way through the puzzle. Follow the words where *th* is pronounced /ð/. Then listen, check and repeat.

↓

brother	both	throat	truth	earth
there	thanks	clothes	them	father
with	sunbathing	together	athlete	although
theatre	bathroom	birthday	breathe	another
third	mouth	healthy	leather	south
thick	threw	thought	rhythm	these

↓

d 🔊 **61** Listen and practise saying these sentences.

There were three earthquakes in the south.

My father and mother both hate this weather.

Catherine can throw the ball further than her brother.

Practise saying these words

🔊 **62** campaign   confusing   detail   diamond
fascinating   gorgeous   hideous   industry   product
shocked   signature   truthful

a Read the text. What is the author's main purpose in writing this article? Choose the best answer: A, B or C.

    A to tell us about Adrian Barker's life

    B to show the skills needed to perform as a 'living statue'

    C to explain why people choose to perform as 'living statues'

A living statue in Barcelona

Living statues

You've probably seen them – those silent performers who look so much like real sculptures that you get a shock when they suddenly move or look into your eyes. They are the street artists who make money by acting as 'living statues' and they can be seen on city streets throughout the world.

If you think this seems like an easy job, think again. Adrian Barker, a regular performer in London, explains: 'You have to learn how to control your body so that it doesn't move and it looks as though you aren't breathing. This requires concentration, but you also must be able to relax or else your body soon begins to hurt. The first 20 minutes of a performance are the hardest. After that you get into a rhythm. It's rather like meditating. Some performers can stand for an hour without closing their eyes and can reduce their heart rate to 24 beats a minute.'

The illusion can be so perfect that people stop and watch in fascination, and there's a wave of laughter when the 'statue' moves, as if it's come to life for a moment. 'It's like magic,' Adrian says. 'Children are sometimes even a bit frightened – they aren't sure if you're human or not.'

The artists spend hours preparing their act. Adrian puts eight coats of paint on his costumes so they look as if they're made of stone or metal. And his hands, neck and face, including the inside of his nose, lips and ears, have to be carefully covered by body paint. It can take up to three hours to get ready for a performance – and another hour to clean up afterwards.

Next year Adrian is hoping to take part in the 'living statues' event which awards a prize for the World Champion Living Statue. Performers from many different countries are invited to enter this competition, which takes place every August in the Dutch city of Arnhem and attracts an audience of over 300,000 people.

b Answer the questions.

1 Where do 'living statues' perform?

....

2 Why do the performers need to concentrate in order to look like statues?

....

....

3 What happens if they can't relax?

....

4 Which of these adjectives describe how the performance seems to people in the audience?

fascinating   annoying   amusing   frightening

....

5 Why does Adrian put so much paint on his clothes?

....

6 Where does he want to go next year?

....

Portfolio 9

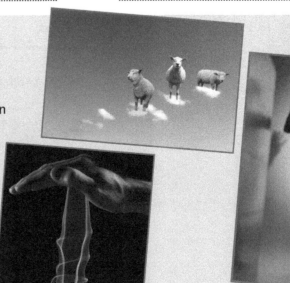

Look at the three photos, which were taken by the finalists in a photography competition on the topic of 'Magic and mystery'.

Paragraphs 1–3
Describe each photo and give your opinion. Use *as if/though* and *like* and some of the adjectives from this unit.

Paragraph 4
Conclusion: say which photo you think should win the competition.

Quiz 9

a What do you remember about Unit 9? Answer all the questions you can and then check in the Student's Book.

A

B

1 Which adjective is the odd one out?

upsetting   amusing   annoying   depressing

2 Circle the correct adjectives.

I love this painting – it's really *shocking / impressive*. The details are *fascinating / confusing* and the colours are *gorgeous / hideous*.

3 Look at picture A. What special skill does this man have?

....

4 Look at picture B and complete the sentences with *as if* and *like*.

The girl seems .... a giant. She looks .... she is touching the top of the man's head. Photos .... this are fun.

5 What sort of image is picture B? Put the letters in order

aclipot lunisoil ....

6 Complete the sentences with *a, an, the* or – (no article).

In ¹........... kitchen at ²........... home we've got ³........... photo of ⁴........... main street in our town. It was taken by ⁵........... architect who went to ⁶........... university with Dad.

7 Add articles to these sentences where they are needed.

Sara Vernet is French painter and she's got exhibition at Museum of Modern Art. I enjoyed exhibition, although I usually prefer paintings with brighter colours.

8 Circle the correct words.

She tried to *fool / forge* us. She said it was a real diamond ring, but that was a *lie / white lie*. We could see the ring was *fake / trick*.

9 Complete the sentences.

A person who tells lies is a l........................... .
A t........................... person tells the truth.

10 Circle the words which have the /θ/ sound (e.g. *three*).

the   thin   then   thanks   healthy
weather   birthday   sunbathe

b 🔊 63 Listen and check your answers.

c Now look at your Student's Book and write three more quiz questions for Unit 9.

Question: ....

Answer: ....

Question: ....

Answer: ....

Question: ....

Answer: ....

10 Beyond words

1 Vocabulary

Reading materials

a Put the letters in order. Write the words and match them with the pictures.

1 hapobyrig .... ☐

2 kobe-o .... ☐

3 nevlo .... ☐

4 peylenarcs .... ☐

5 chipgar volen .... ☐

6 rhilterl .... ☐

b Complete the sentences.

1 Harry, Ron and Hermione are the main characters in the Harry Potter ....s.

2 The dialogue in that film was very clever. Who wrote the ....?

3 I've just read a new ....on the life of Elvis Presley.

4 I'll download this .... , so I can read it on my computer.

5 A good .... always tells an exciting story, with lots of action and adventure.

6 Her .... is fascinating. She gives wonderful descriptions of her life in India.

7 The pictures in a .... novel make it easy to follow the story.

8 I prefer reading .... , because I'm interested in real people and events.

2 Grammar Grammar reference: page 98

Reported statements

> **Check it out!**
>
> **Pronouns and possessive adjectives sometimes have to be changed for reported speech.**
>
> *'We didn't bring our books with us.'*
> They said **they** hadn't brought **their** books with **them**.

a Complete the reported sentences with the correct form of the verb.

1 'I feel sick.'
Matthew said he .... sick.

2 'I wrote a poem about you.'
She said she .... a poem about me.

3 'My sister is performing in a play.'
Eva said her sister .... in a play.

4 'It didn't take long to read the article.'
He said it .... long to read the article.

5 'The tickets will cost a lot of money.'
Nick told us the tickets .... a lot of money.

6 'I've seen the movie twice.'
She said she .... the movie twice.

b Rewrite the speakers' words as reported speech.

1 *I've left my purse at home!* **2** *I'm ready.*

Alice Omar

I can pay for your meal.

Hannah David

I don't think you'll be warm enough.

3 *I'm having trouble with this essay.* **4** *I'm sorry you didn't pass your exam.*

Nadia Carlos

I finished mine yesterday.

Isabel Steve

My parents won't be pleased.

1 Alice said she had left her purse at home.
   Omar said

2

3

4

Help yourself!

Reporting verbs

There are lots of English verbs that we can use instead of *said*. Match these verbs with the meanings. Use your dictionary if you need to.

1 replied ☐   **5** murmured ☐
2 added ☐   **6** shouted ☐
3 repeated ☐   **7** cried ☐
4 whispered ☐   **8** announced ☐

A said extremely loudly
B said something extra
C said in answer to someone
D said extremely quietly
E said formally to give information about plans
F said again
G said quietly and not very clearly
H said loudly with a feeling of pain

---

3 Vocabulary

Adverbs and adverbial phrases

a 🔊 64 Circle the correct words. Then listen and check.

> [1]*At the beginning / At first* of our journey everything seemed perfect. We left Bourke at 8am and [2]*one night / soon afterwards* we turned onto a little road going west. There were no other cars and the countryside was wild and wonderful.
>
> Then, as we passed a group of trees, a huge kangaroo [3]*suddenly / luckily* jumped out in front of us. We didn't hit it, but the car ran off the road and rolled fifteen metres down the hill. We spent an hour trying to push it back up, but it was impossible. [4]*Meanwhile, / Surprisingly,* the sun was getting hotter all the time. There was nothing we could do except wait … and hope.
>
> [5]*Unfortunately, / Eventually,* we heard the sound of a car. It was a farmer on his way home, and he stopped to help us. Together we got the car back onto the road and [6]*fortunately, / meanwhile,* when I turned the key, the engine started. [7]*Soon afterwards, / In the end*, it wasn't a disaster, so we were very lucky!

b Look at the adverbs and adverbial phrases in *italics* in Exercise 3a and find:

1 two expressions that mark the start of a series of events

2 two expressions that mark the end of a series of events

3 an expression that moves the action forward a little in time

4 two expressions that refer to good luck

5 an expression that refers to bad luck

6 an expression for an event that happened quickly and unexpectedly

(4) Grammar Grammar reference: page 98

Reported questions, commands and requests

a Circle the correct answer.

1 We asked them *to want* / *if they wanted* something to eat.

2 Sophie asked me *whether* / *where* I was going to the gym in the afternoon.

3 Mr Fielding told *us to* / *to us* finish the essay at home.

4 I rang Liam last night to ask if *he's* / *he'd* heard the news.

5 Dad told my sister *help* / *to help* with the housework.

6 Tom asked me what *was the time* / *the time was*.

7 I wasn't sure how to do the exercise, so I *asked* / *told* the teacher to help me.

8 We asked the woman in the ticket office how long we *will* / *would* have to wait for the train.

b Complete the reported questions, commands and requests.

Oliver, has the letter arrived?

1 **Rachel:**

Rachel asked Oliver .... the letter

....

Put your bags under your desks.

2 **Miss Neill:**

Miss Neill .... us ....

....

Will you lend me your calculator?

3 **Stefan:**

Stefan .... me ....

....

Clean your room this afternoon, Marta.

4 **Dad:**

Dad ....

....

When will we get our results, Lee?

5 **Emma:**

....

....

Joe, could you carry this box for me?

6 **Mia:**

....

....

Annie, are my magazines on your desk?

7 **Lucas:**

....

....

Reported speech: all forms

c 🔊 65 Complete the dialogues. Change the reported speech to direct speech. Then listen and check.

1 Karen said she couldn't find her phone and asked her brother Tim if he knew where it was. He said he hadn't seen it lately. Karen asked him to help her find it.

Karen: Tim, I .... phone. .... where ....?

Tim: I .... it lately.

Karen: .... it, please?

2 Jack asked Amy what she was doing later that day. Amy said she hadn't made any plans. Jack asked if she wanted to go and see the new *Star Trek* film. Amy thanked him, but said she had seen it the previous day. She told him to go and see it anyway. She said she was sure he would enjoy it.

Jack: Amy, what ....?

Amy: .... any plans.

Jack: .... the new *Star Trek* film?

Amy: Oh, no thanks, Jack. I .... But .... it anyway. I ....

5 Listen

a 🔊 66 Listen to the four conversations. Tick (✓) the correct answer: A, B or C.

1 What have they just been doing?

A ☐ B ☐ C ☐

3 Who is the main character in Danny's story?

A ☐ B ☐ C ☐

2 What kind of book are they talking about?

A ☐ B ☐ C ☐

4 Which section of the shop does the boy need?

A ☐ B ☐ C ☐

b 🔊 66 Listen again and complete the sentences using reported speech.

1 Mike said he thought Christopher Nolan ....

2 The boy asked Jane to ....

3 Kate asked Danny what ....

4 The woman told Stephen to ....

6 Pronunciation

Rhythm

> **Check it out!**
>
> *yonder* = over there   *Ethiop* = Ethiopian
> *bonny* = lovely   *lass* = girl
>
> The words *doth* (= does), *thou/thee* (= you) and *art* (= are) are old forms of English which are not used now.

a 🔊 67 Listen to these lines by Romeo in *Romeo and Juliet*. Then listen again and repeat.

But, <u>soft</u>! what <u>light</u> through <u>yon</u>der <u>win</u>dow <u>breaks</u>?
It is the <u>east</u>, and <u>Ju</u>liet is the <u>sun</u> …

<u>O</u>! she doth <u>teach</u> the <u>tor</u>ches to <u>burn</u> <u>bright</u>.
It <u>seems</u> she <u>hangs</u> upon the <u>cheek</u> of <u>night</u>
Like a <u>rich</u> <u>jewel</u> in an <u>Ethiop</u>'s <u>ear</u>.

b 🔊 68 Listen to these lines from a poem by the Scottish poet Robert Burns. <u>Underline</u> the stressed syllables. Then listen again and check.

O, my love's like a red, red rose
That's newly sprung in June.
O, my love's like the melody
That's sweetly played in tune.

As fair art thou, my bonny lass,
So deep in love am I,
And I will love thee still, my dear,
Till all the seas go dry.

Robert Burns, 1794

> **Practise saying these words**
>
> 🔊 69 biography   castle   enemy
> eventually   imaginary   novel   original
> playwright   publish   recommendation
> thriller   unfortunately

7 Read

a Read the story of *Romeo and Juliet* and complete it with the words in the box.

> later that night   immediately   Meanwhile
> One evening   In the end   Soon afterwards
> On the night before her wedding

Romeo and Juliet a summary

The play takes place in Verona, Italy. Romeo and Juliet are two teenagers whose families, the Montagues and the Capulets, are enemies. Fighting often breaks out between the two families, although the Prince of Verona has told them to keep the peace.

¹..................................., Juliet's parents have a party at their house. One of the guests is Paris, a young man who wants to marry Juliet, with her parents' agreement. But Romeo also decides to come to the party, uninvited. When he and Juliet see each other, they ²................................... fall in love. Meeting again at her window ³..................................., they promise each other that they will get married. The next day, a priest, Friar Laurence, agrees to help them, and so the young lovers marry secretly, without the knowledge of their families.

⁴..................................., their difficulties get worse. In a street fight, Romeo's best friend is killed by Juliet's cousin Tybalt, and Romeo then kills Tybalt in return. For this crime, the Prince orders Romeo to leave Verona. ⁵..................................., Juliet's father has already set a date for her marriage to Paris and will not listen when she tries to break the arrangement.

Juliet is desperate, but Friar Laurence has a plan. He gives her a bottle containing a powerful drug. When she drinks it, it will make her look as though she is dead. After she has been put in the family tomb, she will wake up again. Friar Laurence will send a message to Romeo, who will come and take her away with him.

⁶..................................., Juliet drinks from the bottle and the plan seems to be working well. But Romeo doesn't get the message from Friar Laurence. He hears the news that Juliet has died and thinks it is true. He returns to Verona, goes to the Capulet tomb and takes poison. When Juliet wakes, she finds her husband dead beside her, and she also kills herself.

⁷..................................., the two enemy families come together at last, sharing the pain of losing the two children they loved.

b Answer the questions.

1 Where do Romeo and Juliet first meet?

....

2 Why do they have to keep their love secret?

....

3 Who knows about their marriage?

....

4 Why is Romeo sent away from Verona?

....

5 What does Juliet's father want her to do?

....

6 What is the effect of the drug that Friar Laurence gives her?

....

7 Why doesn't the plan work?

....

8 Why does Juliet kill herself?

....

Portfolio 10

Tell the story of a piece of fiction that you have read and liked. It could be:
- a novel
- a play
- a short story
- a graphic novel

Include only the most important events and use time expressions (adverbs and adverbial phrases) to move the story along.

Check it out!

Remember, we use the present simple as the main tense when we tell the story of a book or film.

Quiz 10

a What do you remember about Unit 10? Answer all the questions you can and then check in the Student's Book.

1 **Choose the correct ending.**

The girl in picture A has been reading

A a manga story.

B an online magazine.

C a blog.

2 **What is Romeo's family name?**

....

3 **Make four words connected with reading.**

thrill non- book graphy fiction
e- bio er

....

....

4 **Choose the correct answer: A, B or C.**

A character is ...

A an exciting novel.   **B** a fictional person.

C a type of poem.

5 **Use both boxes to make five time phrases.**

soon one | end afterwards
in the at at the | beginning first day

....

....

....

6 **Choose the correct words.**

Helen *said / told* she *wants / wanted* to see me and she *will / would* meet me at 5 o'clock.

7 **Complete the reported sentences.**

'I've tried to read this book, but I can't finish it.'

Adam said .... ,

but ....

8 **One sentence is incorrect.** ~~Cross out~~ **the wrong words and write the correct ones.**

A I asked her if she was feeling better.

B I asked her to help me.

C I asked her what was she doing.

....

9 **Look at picture B and complete the reported speech.**

Ellie's father asked her ....

.... and told her ....

.... immediately.

10 **Underline** **the stressed syllables in these lines.**

A lovely young woman called Jane,
Had a wonderful journey through Spain,
She balanced a rose,
On the end of her nose,
And then danced with a man in the rain.

b 🔊 **70** Listen and check your answers.

c Now look at your Student's Book and write three more quiz questions for Unit 10.

Question: ....

....

Answer: ....

Question: ....

....

Answer: ....

Question: ....

....

Answer: ....

11 Is it a crime?

1 Vocabulary

Crime

a Put the boxes in order and write the words for crimes.

bur	tin	aris
ing	eft p	plif
ack	g van	ry th
dali	glar	m pir
lagi	bbe	y sho
acy h	sm ro	

1 burglary   5 ....
2 sho............   6 ....
3 .... 7 ....
4 .... 8 ....

b Look at the word in **bold**. If it is correct, tick (✓) the sentence. If it is wrong, ~~cross it out~~ and write the correct word.

1 Our teachers tell us not to **plagiarist** material from the internet.
....

2 I was very upset about the **theft** of my watch. ....

3 **Vandalises** have broken a lot of the seats in the park. ....

4 The **shoplift** was caught as she tried to leave the shop. ....

5 **Hack** into other people's computers is a serious crime. ....

6 **Pirates** had copied the film and were selling it as a cheap DVD.

7 Someone broke into the shop and **robbed** some valuable jewellery.
....

8 My uncle's house was **burgled** last month.
....

c Complete the sentences.

1 The police are looking for three men who took part in Friday's bank r.. .

2 The t.. stole an mp3 player and some cash from Jack's bag.

3 Last year someone h.. into the company's computer system and destroyed some important files.

4 A p.. is someone who copies other people's ideas.

5 There's a lot of v.. in our town. Buildings are often damaged and there's graffiti everywhere.

6 The organisation was p.. music and selling it illegally.

7 After the b.. we changed all the locks on our doors and windows at home.

8 Most supermarkets have hidden cameras to try to catch s.. .

2 Grammar

Grammar reference: page 100

Subject and object questions

a Read the joke questions and write *S* (subject question) or *O* (object question). Then match the questions with the answers.

1 What has two legs but can't walk? .... [E]
2 What goes up but never comes down? ....S.... [ ]
3 What do sea monsters eat? .... [ ]
4 What city doesn't have any people? .... [ ]
5 What do lazy dogs do for fun? .... [ ]
6 What has many rings but no fingers? .... [ ]
7 What do cats like eating on a hot day? .... [ ]

A They chase parked cars.   E A pair of trousers.
B Mice cream.   F Electricity.
C Your age.   G Fish and ships.
D A telephone.

b (Circle) the correct words.

1 Who *wrote / did write* this article?
2 Where *you go / do you go* for your piano lessons?
3 How many people *invited / did they invite* to the party?
4 What *took / did it take* place here 200 years ago?
5 What creatures *live / do they live* in the desert?
6 Who *this jacket belongs / does this jacket belong* to?
7 How *the police caught / did the police catch* the thieves?
8 Which cable *connects / do you connect* the printer with the computer?

c Complete the questions.

1 A: How much .... (pay) for that shirt?
   B: It cost me £18.

2 A: Which type of animal .... (have) warm blood?
   B: A mammal.

3 A: Oh! What .... (make) that noise?
   B: I think it was just the wind.

4 A: Who .... (like) best in your class?
   B: I like everyone, but Ricardo's my best mate.

5 A: What .... (happen) to water at 0°C?
   B: It freezes.

6 A: How many albums .... (record) in the 1990s?
   B: I think she recorded seven altogether.

7 A: Orlando Bloom is in this film, isn't he? Which part .... (play)?
   B: He's the hero, of course!

8 A: Who .... (steal) your mobile?
   B: I have no idea who it was.

③ Listen

a ◁》 **71** Listen to the two dialogues. Which types of crime are the people talking about? Match the dialogues with the correct pictures.

A

B

C

D

b ◁》 **71** Listen again and answer the questions.

Dialogue 1

1 Where did the crime take place?

....

2 What was Gemma carrying in her hands?

....

3 How many people took part in the theft?

....

4 How much money was stolen?

....

Dialogue 2

5 What was the crime?

....

6 What was taken, as well as electrical equipment?

....

7 What will help the police to catch the criminals?

....

8 How did Jack and his family feel when they got home?

....

(4) Vocabulary

Crime collocations

a Use words from both boxes to make collocations. Write them in the correct part of the table.

arrest do community	prison record
pay commit go to	sentence service
break get a prison	a fine a suspect
get a criminal	a crime with a crime
charge someone	the law

Criminal actions	
Actions taken by police	
Punishments for crime	

b 🔊 72 Complete the text. Write one word in each gap. Then listen and check.

When the police think they know that someone has ¹................ the law, they can ²................ the suspect and take him/her to the police station. If there is enough evidence, they ³................ the person ⁴................ the crime. After that, a judge (and sometimes a jury) usually decides whether the person is guilty or not.

If someone has ⁵................ a crime that isn't very serious, or if they have no previous criminal ⁶................ , the punishment may be light. They might have to ⁷................ a fine, or they might have to do ⁸................ service, which means doing useful unpaid work in their local area. For a more serious crime, the judge may give the criminal a prison ⁹................ . This means the person has to go to ¹⁰................ for a period of time – perhaps for just a few weeks, perhaps for years.

Help yourself!

Homonyms

Homonyms are words that look the same but have different meanings.

Find one word that fits both sentences, a and b.

1 a I had to pay a .... for parking in the wrong place.

b 'How are you today?'
'................ , thanks.'

2 a I have no criminal .... because I've never committed a crime.

b The band has signed a contract with a new .... label.

3 a She received a prison .... of five years.

b Always start a .... with a capital letter.

4 a The police are going to .... him with theft.

b There's no .... for this service – it's free.

5 a The robbers stole thousands of pounds from the ....

b We had a picnic on the .... of the river.

---

(5) Grammar

Grammar reference: page 88

wish and *if only*

a Read the sentences and then decide if the statements below them are *right* (✓) or *wrong* (✗).

1 *I wish the rain would stop.*
It's raining now. ☐

2 *I wish we had less homework.*
We get too much homework. ☐

3 *If only I'd finished my essay!*
I'm happy because I finished my essay. ☐

4 *I wish he wasn't so impatient.*
He's very impatient. ☐

5 *I wish they hadn't broken the window.*
They didn't break the window. ☐

6 *If only our team would win!*
I'm really sorry they didn't win. ☐

b Choose the correct answer: A, B or C.

① If only he _____ !

② I wish I _____ it to the garage.

③ I wish you _____ that jacket all the time.

④ If only I _____ a motorbike!

⑤ If only I _____ my key!

⑥ I wish I _____ Italian.

1	**A** went away	**B** would go away	**C** had gone away
2	**A** took	**B** would take	**C** 'd taken
3	**A** don't wear	**B** wouldn't wear	**C** hadn't worn
4	**A** had	**B** 'd have	**C** 'd had
5	**A** didn't forget	**B** wouldn't forget	**C** hadn't forgotten
6	**A** spoke	**B** would speak	**C** had spoken

c Complete the sentences, using your own ideas.

1 I'm boiling! If only ....
....!

2 My teacher was really angry with me. I wish ....
....

3 We can't go out in this weather. If only ....
....!

4 My friend was extremely upset. I wish ....
....

5 I'm bored. If only ....
....!

(6) Pronunciation
Consonant clusters

a 🔊 **73** Listen and tick (✓) the word you hear.

1 test ☐	text ☐
2 gift ☐	gifts ☐
3 wrist ☐	risked ☐
4 jump ☐	jumped ☐
5 pains ☐	paints ☐
6 subject ☐	subjects ☐
7 relax ☐	relaxed ☐
8 protect ☐	protects ☐

b 🔊 **74** Now listen to these words and tick (✓) the word you hear.

1 state ☐	straight ☐
2 stuck ☐	struck ☐
3 stay ☐	spray ☐
4 contact ☐	contract ☐
5 console ☐	control ☐
6 campaign ☐	complain ☐
7 access ☐	actress ☐
8 except ☐	expect ☐

c 🔊 **75** Listen and practise saying these phrases.

empty hands

strange facts

expensive lipstick

helpful friends

a complete script

an impressive display

Practise saying these words

🔊 **76** apologise burglar
commit criminal identity
illegal licence piracy
plagiarise suspicious thief
vandalism

---

(7) Read

a Read the comments about CCTV (closed circuit TV) security cameras. Write the letters A–E in the correct places (1–5).

A Is it because they've got something to hide?

B What do other people think?

C Who can stop technology from developing and people from using it?

D What's wrong with that?

E Do we really want to live in a society like this?

http://interactive.cambridge.org

paolo51
At my school we've had CCTV security for quite a few years. About 30 cameras were put up, mainly on the outside of the buildings, and I don't mind that so much – I think it's normal, because there are security cameras all round the city now. But recently they've put cameras in the classrooms too, and the school is starting to seem like a prison. My friends feel the same. We don't want to skive off school or behave badly in class, but we hate the feeling that someone is watching us all the time. ^{1}............

JessicaK
I totally agree. It's like they're expecting you to do something wrong, so you feel like a suspect who has to be constantly watched. But it's the same everywhere. There are cameras in the streets,

in shops, in public transport, and now companies are putting them in offices and factories to check up on workers. ^{2}............ We should stop this happening before we lose all our freedom.

wendy
The cameras are there for security. They're there to prevent crime and to catch criminals. In schools the idea is to stop people coming in illegally and to help to prevent theft, vandalism and fighting. ^{3}............ In my school there were lots of problems before we had cameras, but things have improved since then.

kevin007
Why are some people so uncomfortable with CCTV? ^{4}............ If you've done nothing wrong, you've got nothing to worry

about. We've had cameras in our classrooms for ages and the film is only used if there's a problem. It's the same with the cameras in other places. Most of us are in favour of security cameras and don't mind giving up a bit of freedom for better protection. I wish other people would stop complaining and keep quiet!

HanaMac
^{5}............ Just accept it. CCTV is here to stay, and that's only the start. Governments, private companies and criminal organisations can find out all about you if they want to – through your credit cards, your mobile phone, how you use the web and the emails or text messages that you send. You don't like being watched? Tough! Get used to it. That's how things are now.

b Choose the correct answer: A, B or C.

1 Paolo ...

  A doesn't think security is important.

  B accepts some uses of CCTV cameras in schools.

  C wishes that CCTV cameras were banned in schools.

2 Jessica says that ...

  A she has been accused of committing a crime.

  B students are the main targets of CCTV security systems.

  C CCTV reduces people's freedom.

3 Wendy thinks that CCTV cameras ...

  A help to stop people stealing in schools.

  B may be illegal.

  C have resolved all the problems at her school.

4 Kevin thinks that ...

  A only guilty people need to worry about CCTV cameras.

  B there are sometimes problems with the cameras.

  C freedom is more important than protection.

5 Hana ...

  A is excited about the developments in technology.

  B wishes people would make less use of modern technology.

  C doesn't talk about security cameras in schools.

Portfolio 11

Write a discussion essay on this topic:
We should have security cameras in every school and every classroom. Discuss.

Write four paragraphs:

1 introduction

2 arguments in favour of the statement

3 arguments against the statement

4 your conclusion

Quiz 11

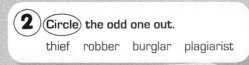

a What do you remember about Unit 11? Answer all the questions you can and then check in the Student's Book.

1 <u>Underline</u> the crime in picture A.

piracy   identity theft   burglary

2 (Circle) the odd one out.

thief   robber   burglar   plagiarist

3 Write the verbs for these nouns.

piracy   ....

robbery   ....

vandalism   ....

4 Which celebrity was the target for a hacker in 2005?

....

5 (Circle) the correct words.

Who *want / wants / do you want* a drink?

What *want you / you want / do you want* to drink?

6 Write the questions. Use the past simple.

Who / go / to the concert?

....

Who / they / see at the concert?

....

7 Look at picture B and (circle) the correct words.

The girl is in a police ¹*house / station* because she ²*broke / committed* the law. The police have ³*arrested / charged* her with vandalism and she will probably have to pay a ⁴*service / fine* of £80.

8 Are these sentences *right (✓)* or *wrong (✗)*?

A The police do community service. ☐

B A person's crimes are listed in their criminal record. ☐

C If you get a prison sentence, you have to go to jail. ☐

9 What does this sentence mean? Choose the best sentence: A, B or C.

If only he played for our team!

A He used to play for our team.

B He doesn't play for our team.

C I'm sorry he doesn't play for our team.

10 Complete the sentence.

These shoes are uncomfortable. I wish I

.... (not buy) them.

b 🔊 **77** Listen and check your answers.

c Now look at your Student's Book and write three more quiz questions for Unit 11.

Question: ....

....

Answer: ....

Question: ....

....

Answer: ....

Question: ....

....

Answer: ....

12 Moving on

1 Grammar Grammar reference: page 100

would rather and would prefer

a Circle the correct words.

1 I'd prefer *go / to go* swimming than play tennis today.

2 He'd rather *live / to live* in the country than in the city.

3 *Would / Do* you rather have tea or coffee?

4 I'd rather you *won't / didn't* tell anyone else about this.

5 I'd prefer *not to / to not* stay out late tonight.

6 Alison would *prefer / rather* to listen to music than study for her exams.

b Make sentences using words from both boxes.

| have | stay | a taxi | different clothes |
| take | he / wear | in bed | a hamburger |

1 Sam / prefer

....

2 I / rather

....

3 They / rather

....

4 Liz / prefer

....

c Complete the sentences so they are true for you.

1 I have to ....
this evening, but I'd prefer ....
....

2 If I was choosing between a trip to the USA and a trip to the UK, I'd rather ....
....

3 I'd rather people didn't ....
.... It annoys me!

Help yourself!

prefer and **would prefer**

Look at these examples.

I **prefer** runn**ing** to exercis**ing** in the gym.
(= a general preference which is true all the time)

I**'d prefer to** have pizza than pasta tonight.
(= a particular preference for something to happen now or in the future)

Complete the sentences. Use *prefer* or *would prefer* and the verb in brackets.

1 A: Do you want to go out later?
B: Actually, I .... (stay) at home this evening.

2 A: Does Javier enjoy playing video games?
B: Yes, but he .... (read).

3 A: Talent shows are fun, aren't they?
B: Sometimes they're OK, but I .... (watch) quiz shows.

4 A: Are you going to make a sandwich?
B: No, I think I .... (have) a bowl of soup.

2 Vocabulary

Hopes and ambitions

a Put the letters in order and write the words in the crossword.

pexcet   ima   eviache   loga
hepo   banimito   eglaneclh

Check it out!

Look at these examples for ways we can use the verbs *aim*, *hope* and *expect*.

I'm aiming I hope I expect	**to** finish	this work by Friday.
I hope I expect (that)	**he will** finish	
I expect	**him to** finish	

b 🔊 78 Choose the correct answer: A, B or C. Then listen and check.

A: Karen ¹.......... to go to university, doesn't she?

B: Yes, and after that she'll probably be really successful. She's got lots of confidence and she's very ².......... .

A: And what about you? What do you want to do in the future?

B: Well, at the moment my ³.......... is to get into the drama academy. There's lots of competition for places, though, so it's going to be a ⁴.......... .

A: Yes, but go for it! It will be a real ⁵.......... if you can get in.

B: Well, that's my ⁶.......... , anyway. My drama teacher thinks I've got a good chance, and I ⁷.......... she's right!

1	A	goals	B	expects	C	achieves
2	A	hoping	B	challenging	C	ambitious
3	A	goal	B	hope	C	expect
4	A	challenge	B	challenged	C	challenging
5	A	ambition	B	achievement	C	aim
6	A	aim	B	expecting	C	ambitious
7	A	hope	B	hoping	C	hoped

3 Grammar   Grammar reference: page 88

Third conditional

a Match the two parts of the sentences.

1 If I'd known it was your birthday yesterday, ☐

2 If Erica had phoned her parents, ☐

3 I couldn't have done my homework if ☐

4 We might have won the match if ☐

5 If Julie hadn't gone to the party, ☐

6 If their bus hadn't been late, ☐

7 It would have been very disappointing if ☐

8 The police wouldn't have arrested him if ☐

A Eduardo had been fit enough to play.

B we hadn't been able to get tickets for the concert.

C they wouldn't have got so worried.

D they would have arrived half an hour ago.

E he hadn't taken part in the robbery.

F I would have bought you a present.

G you hadn't helped me.

H I might never have met her.

b Complete the third conditional sentences with the correct form of the verbs.

1 If it .... (be) warmer yesterday, they .... (go) swimming.

2 If we .... (run) out of petrol, we .... (not know) what to do.

3 If Anna .... (not recommend) the book, I .... (not read) it.

4 I .... (tell) Mike the news last night if I .... (see) him.

5 You .... (not lose) your camera if you .... (be) more careful with it.

6 We .... (not get) into the restaurant last night if we .... (not book) a table.

7 .... you .... (remember) Tom's birthday if I .... (not remind) you?

8 What .... Lisa .... (do) if she .... (not find) her wallet yesterday?

c Look at the completed sentences in Exercise 3b. Are these statements *right* (✓) or *wrong* (✗)?

1 It wasn't warm enough to go swimming yesterday. ☐

2 Luckily, we didn't run out of petrol. ☐

3 I didn't read the book that Anna recommended. ☐

4 I saw Mike last night but I didn't tell him the news. ☐

5 You lost your camera because you weren't careful. ☐

6 Unfortunately, we didn't book a table at the restaurant. ☐

7 I reminded you about Tom's birthday. ☐

8 Lisa's wallet is lost. ☐

④ Vocabulary

Dependent prepositions

a Look at the pictures and make six sentences from the table.

He's interested		winning the prize.
She isn't very good	at	the weekend.
He succeeded	on	playing the violin.
She's concentrating	in	her work.
He isn't keen	to	birds.
She's looking forward		winter sports.

1 ....

2 ....

3 ....

4 ....

5 ....

6 ....

b Complete the sentences.

1 A: Are you .... in Geography?

   B: No, I find it boring.

2 A: Has Grace chosen a present for Mateo?

   B: Yes, she's decided .... a shirt.

3 A: Sandro is making .... in essay writing, isn't he?

   B: Yes, his work is getting better all the time.

4 A: I'm not .... forward .... seeing the dentist.

   B: Stop worrying. It'll be fine.

5 A: Will you turn down the music? I'm trying to .... on my homework.

   B: Sorry!

6 A: After three days, they .... in getting to the top of the mountain.

   B: That was a real achievement!

7 A: Is she a good musician?

   B: She can't play the guitar very well but she's not bad .... singing.

8 A: If he's found guilty, what sentence will he get?

   B: That will .... on the judge.

c Write answers that are true for you.

1 something you have succeeded in

   ....

2 something you have made progress in

   ....

3 an activity you are keen on

   ....

4 an event you are looking forward to

   ....

5 Listen

a 🔊 79 Listen to the conversation between Amy and Luca. Then answer the questions.

1 Who is better at Maths? ....

2 Who is less keen on going to university?

   ....

3 Who had health problems last summer?

   ....

b 🔊 79 Listen again and complete the table. Write your answers in note form.

		Amy	Luca
1	Regrets about the past year		
2	Aims for next year		
3	Goals for later in the future		

6 Pronunciation

Sentence stress

a 🔊 80 Listen and underline the **two** words that are stressed. Then listen again and repeat.

1 I'm interested in science.

2 Are you making progress?

3 It's a stupid idea!

4 They were arguing about money.

5 Is he concentrating on his work?

b 🔊 81 Underline the **three** stressed words. Then listen, check and repeat.

1 Are they going for a walk in the park?

2 Our decision will depend on the weather.

3 There's a serious problem with the computer.

4 How did you know I was at home?

5 If it had rained, we'd have closed the windows.

c 🔊 82 Listen and practise saying these sentences.

Is she happy with her results? *(2 stresses)*

Tell me about your visit to the museum. *(3 stresses)*

He's succeeded brilliantly in his career as an actor. *(4 stresses)*

Where will she be staying when she makes her trip to London? *(5 stresses)*

Practise saying these words

🔊 83 achievement   ambitious   challenge
concentrate   effort   expectation   hopeful
preference   progress   succeed

---

(7) Read

a Read the advert for a competition.
Are these sentences *right* (✓) or *wrong* (✗)?

1 You must write about events that
   happened a year ago. ☐

2 There is a cash prize for the competition. ☐

3 You must send in your entry on 16 June. ☐

This year has had its ups and downs. There have been fun times and difficult times, but three events stand out for me.

The first of these happened early in the football season. At that time I was very fit and I was playing well in the under-18 A team. I was expecting to have a great season and was even hoping to be selected for the Northern Region junior team. Then, during a match in September, another player crashed into me and I fell over. I knew immediately that something serious had happened and at the hospital they told me my leg was broken in two places. So that was the end of my hopes for the football season. It was really frustrating, but I just had to learn to be patient and accept the situation.

On the other hand, I had some good luck in January. I had wanted a new keyboard for ages because my old one had stopped working, but they were all too expensive for me. Then a friend mentioned a new online music shop and I decided to look at their website. It had the keyboard I wanted at less than half price! With some birthday money from my grandparents, I had just enough to buy it. I was lucky, because there was only one left and if I hadn't bought it quickly, someone else certainly would have grabbed it. Since then, I've been experimenting with electronic sounds and I've written some great music.

The third event was a meeting. It wouldn't have happened if my cousin Nick hadn't asked me to help him with some repairs on his scooter three weeks ago. When I arrived at his house, I found that his sister had invited a friend to stay for the weekend. It was Teresa. As soon as we met I knew that I liked her. She was clever but also funny and very easy to talk to, and we got on amazingly well. Since then, we've talked on the internet every day. I'd prefer to see her but she doesn't live near here so it isn't easy. I can't wait for the holidays. I can't wait to see her again.

b Read Greg's competition entry. Are the sentences *right* (✓), *wrong* (✗) or *doesn't say* (–)?

1 Before the match in September, Greg

   A had never been injured before. ☐

   B had achieved his aims in football. ☐

2 If he hadn't broken his leg,

   A he wouldn't have fallen during the match. ☐

   B he might have played in the Northern
       Region team. ☐

3 Greg bought the keyboard quickly because

   A he hadn't used one before. ☐

   B he knew other people would want it. ☐

4 If he hadn't visited the online shop, he

   A wouldn't have been able to buy this keyboard. ☐

   B would have bought a more expensive keyboard. ☐

5 The meeting between Greg and Teresa

   A depended on a request from Nick. ☐

   B was planned by Greg's cousins. ☐

6 Greg

   A enjoys seeing Teresa as often as possible. ☐

   B is looking forward to seeing Teresa again. ☐

Portfolio 12

Write an essay for the competition in Exercise 7. Write four paragraphs.

Paragraph 1
A short introduction

Paragraphs 2–4
One paragraph for each event. Describe:
• what happened and how you felt
• how the event made a change in your life / may influence you in the future

Quiz 12

a What do you remember about Unit 12? Answer all the questions you can and then check in the Student's Book.

1 (Circle) the correct words.

A: [1]Did / Would you [2]prefer / rather to have lunch here or in the garden?

B: I think [3]I / I'd [4]prefer / rather sit outdoors.

2 Complete the sentence.

I'd rather you .... (not smoke) in here. I don't like the smell.

3 Look at picture A. What is she good at and what is she aiming to do?

....
....

4 (Circle) the odd one out.

goal   aim   progress   ambition

5 Complete the sentences with words for hopes and ambitions.

The snowboarding event is very difficult, so it's going to be a real [1]c... . I don't [2]e... to win but if I could come third or fourth, that would be a great [3]a... for me.

b 🔊 84 Listen and check your answers.

c Now look at your Student's Book and write three more quiz questions for Unit 12.

6 Look at picture B. What two events were they celebrating?

....
....

7 Choose the correct answer: A, B or C.

Suzie passed all her exams, but if she [1]........... more time studying, she [2]........... better results.

1   A spends   B had spent
    C would have spent

2   A got   B would get   C would have got

8 Read the sentence and then tick (✓) the correct statement(s).

I might have taken some photos if my phone hadn't run out of battery.

A   I took some photos. ☐

B   I didn't take any photos. ☐

C   I had planned to take some photos. ☐

D   My phone was working. ☐

E   My phone wasn't working. ☐

9 Match the verbs with the prepositions.

succeed	at
look forward	in
be good	on
depend	to

10 <u>Underline</u> the stressed words in this sentence.

We're organising a special party for the last day of term.

Question: ....
....
Answer: ....

Question: ....
....
Answer: ....

Question: ....
....
Answer: ....

Grammar reference

1 Present simple, present continuous, present perfect

Present simple and present continuous

Present simple	Present continuous
I often **play** video games.	They aren't here, they**'re playing** tennis this afternoon.
It **gets** very cold here in the winter.	Let's go inside now. It**'s getting** cold.
Diana **doesn't work** on Sundays.	She **isn't working** today.
Do you **watch** horror films?	What **are** you **watching** at the moment?

- We use the present simple for permanent situations, regular or repeated actions, and facts. We also use it to describe events in a book or film.

- We use the present continuous for actions happening now and for temporary actions.

- We also use the present continuous for future arrangements. For notes on this use, see page 82.

- We don't normally use the continuous form for these verbs:

like   love   hate   prefer   want   need   know   believe   understand   agree   belong   own   mean

Present perfect

I/You/We/They	've (have)	begun.	I/You/We/They	haven't (have not)	begun.
He/She/It	's (has)		He/She/It	hasn't (has not)	
Have	I/you/we/they	begun?	Yes, I/you/we/they **have**.	No, I/you/we/they **haven't**.	
Has	he/she/it		Yes, he/she/it **has**.	No, he/she/it **hasn't**.	

- The present perfect always makes a connection between the past and the present.

- We use the present perfect to talk about actions at some time in the past up to now. We don't say exactly when they happened.
  She**'s sent** me three text messages today.
  (= from the start of the day up to now)
  Have you ever **been** to Ireland? (= at any time in your life up to now?)

> ✱ Adverbs of frequency go before the past participle.
> *Ben has **never** been to Italy.*
> *I've **often** bought things on the internet.*

- We also use the present perfect for past actions that directly affect the present. They are often recent events.
  Someone **has taken** my bag! (It isn't here now!)
  Has he **bought** the tickets? (Does he have them now?)

> ✱ For irregular past participles, see page 102.

Present perfect with *for* and *since*

- We use the present perfect with *for* and *since* for actions that started in the past and are still happening.
  She**'s known** Stefan **for** five years. (She still knows him now.)
  We**'ve been** here **since** ten o'clock. (We're still here now.)

- We use *for* + a period of time. We use *since* + a point in time when the action began.

Present perfect with *just*, *already* and *yet*

- We use *just* for actions that have happened very recently.
  Matt **has just gone** out. He left five minutes ago.

- We use *already* for actions that have happened sooner than expected.
  A: *Don't forget to send those photos to Sam.*   B: *I've **already sent** them.*

- We use *yet* for actions that are expected. It is used in negative sentences and questions.
  A: **Have** you **finished** the cleaning **yet**?   B: No, we **haven't started** it **yet**.

- *Just* and *already* normally go before the past participle. *Yet* normally goes at the end of the sentence.

Grammar practice

1 Present simple, present continuous, present perfect

a Complete the email with the present simple or present continuous form of the verbs.

> ◄► C ⌂ [   ] — ☐ ✕
>
> Hi Lucy
>
> Grrr! I **1**.................................(feel) a bit fed up right now. My brothers are upstairs and they **2**...........................(shout) at each other, as usual. Every day they **3**.........................(have) a big argument about something, and then of course Mum **4**.............................(get) cross. Meanwhile, Jessica **5**...........................(not speak) to me at the moment because she **6**...........................(think) I broke her necklace. I didn't! I keep telling her I **7**...........................(not know) how it broke, but she **8**...........................(not believe) me.
>
> Anyway, how are you? **9**..............you still ....(want) to come for a visit next weekend?
>
> I **10**.......................(look) forward to seeing you.
>
> Martina xx

b Choose the correct answers: A, B or C.

			A	B	C
1	Karen .... stayed in this hotel before.		hasn't	wasn't	didn't
2	Have you ever .... a horse?		rode	riding	ridden
3	I've had a sore throat .... two days.		ago	for	since
4	Tom isn't here now. He's .... to the cinema.		been	gone	went
5	We've known each other .... 2008.		in	for	since
6	I've .... seen that film. It was on TV a few months ago.		already	just	yet

c Write the sentences. Use the present perfect and add *just, yet* or *already*.

1 A: That's Claudia's cousin. *He / move / here from Barcelona.* — He's just moved here from Barcelona.

   B: *Yes, I / meet / him.* He was at Claudia's house last Sunday. ....

2 A: *You / not cook / anything!* ....

   B: No. *Mum / make / some soup.* It's in the freezer. ....

3 A: *They / arrive / at the airport?* ....

   B: Yes! *The plane / land.* The passengers are getting off now. ....

4 A: *Jack / start / his History essay?* ....

   B: *He / finish / it!* He wrote it last weekend. ....

d Complete the questions using present tenses. Then match them with the answers.

1 ....(Tom / study) at home today? ☐ **A** Yes, a few times.

2 ....(you / ever / try) bungee jumping? ☐ **B** Twice a week.

3 How often ....(they / have) music lessons? ☐ **C** Yes, it's delicious.

4 What ....(you / do) at the moment? ☐ **D** Yes, he does.

5 ....(anyone / taste) the dessert yet? ☐ **E** No, he's at the library.

6 ....(your dad / usually / drive) to work? ☐ **F** I'm watching a DVD.

Grammar reference

(2) Present perfect continuous

I/You/We/They	've (have)	been waiting.	I/You/We/They	haven't (have not)	been waiting.
He/She/It	's (has)		He/She/It	hasn't (has not)	
Have	I/you/we/they	been waiting?	Yes, I/you/we/they **have**. No, I/you/we/they **haven't**.		
Has	he/she/it		Yes, he/she/it **has**. No, he/she/it **hasn't**.		

- For the present perfect continuous we use *have/has + been* + verb with *-ing*.

- We use the present perfect continuous for actions that have been in progress over a period of time up to now. The action may have recently finished or it may still be happening now.

  *I'm taking a break. I***'ve been working*** hard all morning.*
  *Eva **has been talking** on the phone for over an hour.*
  *Our team **hasn't been playing** well lately.*
  *What **have** you **been doing** since I last saw you?*

(3) Past simple and past continuous

Past simple	Past continuous
We **walked** to school yesterday.	This time yesterday we **were walking** on the beach.
He **went** home early on Saturday.	I saw Leo in Park Street. He **was going** to the market.
I **didn't work** hard enough last term.	I couldn't call you because my phone **wasn't working**.
Did you **do** well in your exams?	What **were** you **doing** at lunch time yesterday?

- We use the past simple for completed actions in the past. It is often used with past time expressions like *yesterday*, *last week*, *two days ago*, *in 2008*, etc.

  ✱ For irregular past simple verbs see page 102.

- We use the past continuous for actions that were in progress over a period of time in the past. It often describes what was happening at a certain time.

- We often use the past simple and past continuous together. The past continuous action is longer and started earlier. It was already in progress when the past simple action happened.

  *They **were watching** the news on TV when we **arrived**.*
  *While I **was walking** home, it **started** to rain.*
  *She **broke** her finger while she **was playing** basketball.*
  *When the volcano **erupted**, lots of people **were living** nearby.*

- We can use *when* with both these tenses. However, we normally use *while* only with the past continuous, not with the past simple.

Grammar practice

Present perfect continuous

a Complete the sentences with the present perfect continuous form of the verbs.

wait   do   plan   wear   not listen   not feel

1 I .... glasses since I was eight years old.
2 Nadia is going to see the doctor. She .... well lately.
3 The bus must come soon. How long .... we ....?
4 Concentrate, please, Alex! You .... to me.
5 Marco has booked his flight to New Zealand. He .... this trip for ages.
6 Your clothes are all dirty! What .... you ....?

b (Circle) the correct words.

1 I've already *sent / been sending* Ellie a text message.
2 Steve has *done / been doing* his homework since eight o'clock.
3 The film has just *ended / been ending*.
4 I'm tired now. I've *cleaned / been cleaning* my room all morning.
5 Oh, there you are! Where have you *hidden / been hiding*?
6 Have you *seen / been seeing* a play at this theatre before?

3 Past simple and past continuous

Write sentences. Use one verb in the past simple and the other in the past continuous.

1 Julia / arrive / while we / have lunch

   ....

2 The two men / run away / when the police / catch / them

   ....

3 It / not rain / when I / leave / home this morning

   ....

4 you / buy / any butter when / you / shop / yesterday?

   ....

5 He / play / loud music, so he / not hear / the phone

   ....

6 We / not see / the interview because we / not watch / TV

   ....

Grammar reference

4 used to

I/You/We/They/He/She/It	used to	play.		I/You/We/They/He/She/It	didn't (did not) use to	play.
Did	I/you/we/they/he/she/it	use to	play?	Yes, I/you/we/they/he/she/it **did**. No, I/you/we/they/he/she/it **didn't**.		

- We use *used to / didn't use to* + infinitive for normal or repeated actions in the past. The actions don't happen now.

  I **used to ride** my bike everywhere when I was younger.

  She **didn't use to get** much exercise, but now she goes for a run every day.

  How **did** people **use to travel** in the 19th century?

5 Past perfect

I/You/We/They/He/She/It	'd (had)	spoken.		I/You/We/They/He/She/It	hadn't (had not)	spoken.
Had	I/you/we/they/he/she/it	spoken?		Yes, I/you/we/they/he/she/it **had**. No, I/you/we/they/he/she/it **hadn't**.		

- For the past perfect we use *had* + past participle.

- The past perfect is used when we are already talking about a time in the past. We use it to describe a completed action that happened before that time.

  ✱ For irregular past participles see page 102.

  When we woke up, everything was white. It **had snowed** during the night.

  I enjoyed talking to your brother last night. I **hadn't met** him before.

  The house was empty. Where **had** everyone **gone**?

- *Already*, *just* and adverbs of frequency (*never*, *often*, etc.) go before the past participle.

  By the time she got to the café, her friends **had already left**.

  The meal was amazing. I**'d never tasted** such delicious food.

6 Past perfect continuous

I/You/We/They/He/She/It	'd (had)	been speaking.	I/You/We/They/He/She/It	hadn't	been speaking.
Had	I/you/we/they/he/she/it	been speaking?	Yes, I/you/we/they/he/she/it **had**. No, I/you/we/they/he/she/it **hadn't**.		

- For the past perfect continuous we use *had* + *been* + verb with *-ing*.

- We use the past perfect continuous for an action that was in progress over a period of time before a later event happened. We are showing that the earlier action continued for some time.

  The bus finally arrived at 8:30. We**'d been waiting** at the bus stop for half an hour.

  Lara was tired when she got home. She**'d been studying** at the library since lunch time.

  He **hadn't been driving** for long when he lost his driving licence.

  A: They sold their flat two months ago. B: How long **had** they **been living** there?

- We often use the past perfect continuous with *for* or *since*.

Grammar practice

4 used to

Look at the underlined verbs. If we can replace the past simple with *used to*, write the correct form of *used to*. If we can't replace it with *used to*, write **X**.

1 Monika <u>had</u> blonde hair when she was a baby. ......used to have..
2 Andrew got dressed quickly and <u>ran</u> downstairs. ....
3 In 1995 my aunt and uncle <u>moved</u> to the USA. ....
4 When I was growing up, there <u>weren't</u> many shops in our street. ....
5 In the 19th century no one <u>wore</u> shorts or T-shirts. ....
6 When <u>did you lose</u> your wallet? ....
7 How <u>did people communicate</u> before phones were invented? ....

5 Past perfect

a Complete the sentences with the past perfect form of the verbs.

1 We were a bit late. When we got to the cinema, the film .... (start).
2 Her jumper looked a lot better after she .... (wash) it.
3 It was wonderful to meet Sergio again. I .... (not see) him for years.
4 .... the rain .... (stop) by the time you left this morning?
5 They .... (not go) to London before, and they really enjoyed exploring it.

b Complete the text. Use the past simple or past perfect form of the verbs.

| go | fall | wake up | arrive | not get | already/take | never/see |

My first morning in Mumbai was amazing. My father and I ¹........................ late the night before, and I ²........................ asleep as soon as we got to the hotel room. When I ³........................ at about nine o'clock the next morning, Dad was having a shower. I ⁴........................ to the window and looked out. I ⁵........................ such a crowded, colourful and fascinating street before. By the time Dad came in, I still ⁶........................ dressed and I ⁷........................ about 20 photos.

6 Past perfect continuous

(Circle) the correct words.

1 Ricardo was really wet. He'd *stood / been standing* in the rain for 20 minutes.
2 Lily was Rosa's friend. They'd *known / been knowing* each other since they were in primary school.
3 I was upset when I lost my ring. My grandma had *given / been giving* it to me.
4 Luis didn't get home until dinner time. He'd *trained / been training* with the hockey team since 4:30.
5 Before the electricity was cut off, I'd *chatted / been chatting* to my friends online.
6 The DVD player stopped working three days after we'd *bought / been buying* it!
7 How long had you *had / been having* that video camera?
8 That woman had *stood / been standing* outside our house for 20 minutes!

Grammar reference

7 *will*

I/You/We/They/ He/She/It	**'ll (will)**	**come**.	I/You/We/They/ He/She/It	**won't (will not)**	**come**.
Will	I/you/we/they/ he/she/it	**come**?	Yes, I/you/we/they/he/she/it **will**. No, I/you/we/they/he/she/it **won't**.		

● *Will* is a modal verb which refers to the future. The form *will* + infinitive is the same for all subjects.

● We use *will/won't* to make predictions about the future. The verbs *think*, *suppose*, *believe*, *hope*, *expect* and adverbs like *maybe*, *perhaps* and *probably* are often used with *will* predictions.

*In the future, computers **will be** much faster.*   *I think you**'ll like** this song.*
*It probably **won't rain** on Saturday.*   *Where **will** we **be** in ten years' time?*

● We also use *will/won't* for decisions made at the time of speaking. The decision may be an offer or a promise.

*We need Ben's opinion. I**'ll send** him a text message.*   *I **won't buy** that shirt. It's too expensive.*
*You're cold! I**'ll lend** you a jumper.*   *Jenny has promised that she **won't let** us **down**.*

8 *going to*

I	**'m (am)**			I	**'m not (am not)**		
He/She/It	**'s (is)**	**going to**	**work**.	He/She/It	**isn't (is not)**	**going to**	**work**.
You/We/They	**'re (are)**			You/We/They	**aren't (are not)**		
Am	I			Yes, I **am**.		No, I**'m not**.	
Is	he/she/it	**going to**	**work**?	Yes, he/she/it **is**.		No, he/she/it **isn't**.	
Are	you/we/they			Yes, you/we/they **are**.		No, you/we/they **aren't**.	

● We use *going to* for plans and intentions.

*Danny has gone to the shops. He**'s going to buy** some new jeans.*
*We **aren't going to invite** Klara to the party.*
*I**'m going to get up** earlier from now on.*
*I like your new poster. Where **are** you **going to put** it?*

> ✱ *Will* and *going to* predictions are similar and often both forms are correct. However, if the prediction is given as someone's personal feeling or opinion, we normally use *will*.

● We also use *going to* for predictions based on present evidence. We are very certain that the prediction is accurate – it seems that the action <u>must</u> happen in the future.

*The temperature's going down. It**'s going to be** very cold tonight.*
*It's already five to eight. We **aren't going to get** there on time.*

9 Present continuous for future arrangements

● We can use the present continuous to talk about future arrangements, often for the near future. The future event has already been organised.

*I**'m meeting** Ali for lunch at 12:30.*
*We**'re having** an English test on Friday.*
*She **isn't working** tomorrow – it's a holiday.*
*What time **is** the race **starting**?*

> ✱ Future arrangements with the present continuous are often very similar to plans with *going to* and both forms may be correct.
>
> *I'm **meeting / going to meet** Ali at 12:30.*
>
> However, for an intention with no definite arrangement, we can't use the present continuous.
>
> *I'm **going to work** hard next term. (not ~~I'm working~~)*

Grammar practice

7 will

Use the verbs with *will/won't* to complete the sentences and write *P* (prediction) or *D* (decision).

| be | find | hurt | go | have | make |

1 I'm tired now. I think I ....
............................to bed. ☐

2 Don't worry about the dentist. He
.... you! ☐

3 Do you want something to drink?
I think I ....some tea. ☐

4 I don't think I ....able
to finish this work for Monday. ☐

5 I ....a dessert. Just
a cup of coffee, please. ☐

6 I've looked everywhere for my earring.
I probably ....it now. ☐

8 going to

a Look at the sentences with *going to* and write
I (intention or plan) or *P* (prediction).

1 Be careful! You're going to drop those plates. ☐

2 The car is out of control. It's going to crash! ☐

3 No more chocolate for me! I'm going to lose
some weight this year. ☐

4 Are you going to come by train or by bus? ☐

5 There's almost no one here. It's not going
to be a very good party. ☐

6 Teresa isn't going to watch TV. She wants
to finish her painting. ☐

b Complete the sentences with the correct form
of *will* or *be going to*.

1 Thomas is on his way to Madrid. He
.... (stay) there for
a few days.

2 It's 23° and the sun is shining! It ....
(be) a lovely day.

3 The books I ordered haven't arrived yet. Maybe
they ....(come)
tomorrow.

4 The meal ....probably
.... (be) ready to be served in
about five minutes.

5 They're repairing my disk drive now. I hope it
.... (not cost) a lot.

6 I .... (not clean) my
room today. I've decided to do it tomorrow.

9 Present continuous for future arrangements

Choose the correct answer: A or B.

Eva: What ¹.......... this evening, Lee?

Lee: Nothing much. I'm ².......... to finish
redesigning my website some
time this weekend, but ³.......... that
tomorrow.

Eva: Well, Charlie and I ⁴.......... to a comedy
show at the Playhouse this evening and
we've got an extra ticket. Do you want
to come?

Lee: That sounds good. What time ⁵..........?

Eva: Soon! ⁶.......... at 7:30 outside the theatre.
Can you get there in time?

Lee: Yes, I think so. ⁷.......... the 7:10 bus if I can.

Eva: Right. If you can't get there by 7:30,
⁸.......... your ticket at the box office, OK?

Lee: OK. See you soon.

1	**A** will you do	**B** are you doing
2	**A** going to try	**B** trying
3	**A** I'll probably do	**B** I'm probably doing
4	**A** will go	**B** are going
5	**A** will you leave	**B** are you leaving
6	**A** We'll meet	**B** We're meeting
7	**A** I'll get	**B** I'm going to get
8	**A** we'll leave	**B** we're leaving

Grammar reference

(10) Future continuous

I/You/We/They/He/She/It	'll (will)	be coming.	I/You/We/They/He/She/It	won't (will not)	be coming.
Will	I/you/we/they/he/she/it	be coming?	Yes, I/you/we/they/he/she/it **will**. No, I/you/we/they/he/she/it **won't**.		

- For the future continuous we use *will* + *be* + verb with *-ing*. The form is the same for all subjects.

- We use the future continuous for actions that will be in progress at a time in the future.
  *In a few years' time Beth **will be earning** a lot of money.*
  *This time tomorrow we**'ll be flying** to Greece.*
  *I can't go out on Saturday. I**'ll be studying** for my exams all weekend.*
  *What **will** you **be doing** at midnight on New Year's Eve?*

- We also use the future continuous for things that we expect to happen or intend to do in the future.
  *We**'ll be seeing** Rachel at the meeting tomorrow.*
  *My grandparents **will be arriving** on Tuesday.*
  *I **won't be watching** the match on Saturday. I hate football!*
  *What time **will** you **be leaving**?*

> ✱ When used like this, the future continuous has almost the same meaning as the present continuous for arrangements or *going to* for intentions.
> *We**'re seeing** Rachel at the meeting tomorrow.*
> *My grandparents **are arriving** on Tuesday.*
> *I**'m not going to watch** the match on Saturday.*
> *What time **are** you **going to leave**?*

(11) *if, when, as soon as* and *unless*: future use

***When** he **gets** to King's Cross, he'll have to change trains.*
*The tennis match will continue **as soon as** it **stops** raining.*
*I won't leave **unless** you **come** with me / **if** you **don't come** with me.*

- We can use *when, as soon as, if* and *unless* to talk about the future. The following verb is in the present simple, although it refers to the future.

> ✱ *Before* and *until* also follow this rule.
> *I'll ring you **before** the class **starts**.*
> *I won't be happy **until I see** you again.*

- *As soon as* means 'immediately when'. When we use *when* and *as soon as*, we are sure that the action will happen in the future.

- *Unless* means 'if not'. When we use *if* and *unless*, we aren't sure if the action will happen or not. (See First conditional on page 86.)

Grammar practice

10 Future continuous

a Complete the sentences with the future continuous form of the verbs.

wear   relax   stay   do   have   wait

1 I .... at the station when you get off the train.

2 How long .... they .... in London?

3 You'll be able to find Ryan at the café at about 1pm. He .... lunch there.

4 This time next week Marta .... on the beach.

5 You'll know me when you see me. I .... a red shirt and a baseball cap.

6 From 21 June to 3 July we .... our exams.

b (Circle) the correct answers.

1 When your plane arrives, we'll *wait / be waiting* at the airport to meet you.

2 You must be thirsty. I'll *get / be getting* you something to drink.

3 By the time you get this postcard, I'll probably *travel / be travelling* somewhere in Turkey.

4 This time tomorrow my sister will be in the exam room. She'll *do / be doing* her History exam.

5 In the future, scientists will *understand / be understanding* more about how the human brain works.

11 *if, when, as soon as* and *unless*: future use

Make sentences about the future. Use the words in brackets.

1 We / not be / here – you arrive (when)

....

2 I / not enjoy / the party – you / be / there (unless)

....

3 I / get / some information – I / send / you a text (as soon as)

....

4 Susana / go / for a walk – she / take / the dog with her (if)

....

5 you / try / harder – you / not succeed (unless)

....

6 We / have / dinner – Dad / get / home (as soon as)

....

Grammar reference

(12) First and second conditionals

First conditional

Condition		Result
If	I **have** enough money,	I'**ll** (**will**) **buy** some new headphones.
	he **doesn't pass** his exam,	he'**ll** (**will**) **be** upset.
	you **decide** to do this course,	you **won't** (**will not**) **regret** it.
	it **rains** this evening,	**will** we **stay** at home?

- We use the first conditional to talk about possible situations in the future. The action depends on a condition that is possible but not certain.

  *If I **see** Alice, I'**ll give** her your message.* (Maybe I'll see her – it's possible.)

- In the *if* clause we use a present simple verb, although it refers to the future. In the result clause, we use *will/won't* + infinitive.

- Instead of *if* + *not*, we can use *unless*.

  ***If** the taxi **doesn't come** soon,*
  ***Unless** the taxi **comes** soon,* } *we'll be late for the concert.*

- We can change the order of the two clauses.

  I'll give Alice your message if I see her.
  We'll be late for the concert unless the taxi comes soon.

> ✱ We can use *might* or *may* instead of *will* if we are more uncertain about the result.

Second conditional

Condition		Result
If	I **won** the lottery,	I'**d** (**would**) travel around the world.
	he **worked** harder,	he'**d** (**would**) get better results.
	we **didn't** get any exercise,	we **wouldn't** (**would not**) keep fit.
	you **were** in my situation,	what **would** you **do**?

- We use the second conditional when we are imagining an unreal situation now or in the future. The action depends on a condition that is impossible or unlikely.

  *If I **had** Tony's number, I'**d call** him.* (But I don't have his number, so this is not a possibility.)
  *We'**d be** in trouble if we **ran** out of petrol.* (But we probably won't run out, so this is unlikely.)

- In the *if* clause we use a past simple verb, although it refers to the present or future. In the result clause, we use *would/wouldn't* + infinitive.

> ✱ We can use *might* instead of *would* if we are more uncertain about the result.

- When the verb in the *if* clause is *be*, we can use *I/he/she/it **were*** instead of *was*. This is usual when the subject is *I*.

  *If I **were** you, I'd see a doctor.*
  *If Liz **weren't** (or **wasn't**) so shy, she'd make friends more easily.*

- We can change the order of the two clauses.

  I'd call Tony if I had his number.
  I'd see a doctor if I were you.

Grammar practice

12 First and second conditionals

a Complete the first conditional sentences with the correct form of the verbs.

1 If Jim .... (catch) the 5:15 bus, he .... (get) here before six o'clock.

2 The kitchen .... (be) cooler if we .... (open) the windows.

3 You .... (hurt) yourself with that knife if you .... (not be) careful.

4 If they .... (not read) the instructions, they .... (not know) what to do.

5 What .... we .... (do) if it .... (not stop) raining?

6 If Chloe .... (want) to borrow your bike, ... you ....
(lend) it to her?

b There is a mistake in each of these second conditional sentences. C̶r̶o̶s̶s̶ ̶o̶u̶t̶ the wrong word(s) and write the correct word(s).

1 If he'll speak more clearly, we'd be able to understand him. ....

2 José went to the music festival if he had enough money. ....

3 If birds didn't have wings, they won't be able to fly. ....

4 She isn't such a good swimmer if she didn't train regularly. ....

5 I wouldn't buy that album if I was you. ....

6 If they didn't improve the roads, there wouldn't be so many accidents. ....

c Tick (✓) the correct meaning: A or B.

1 If I see Maria this evening, I'll tell her the news.

   A I expect to see Maria. ☐

   B I'll definitely see Maria. ☐

2 He'd look better if his hair was shorter.

   A He's going to have a haircut soon. ☐

   B He probably won't change his hairstyle. ☐

3 Will we go if they invite us?

   A It's quite likely that we'll get an invitation. ☐

   B I don't think they want us to come. ☐

4 If the weather wasn't so bad, we could have a game of tennis.

   A We'll play tennis when the weather improves. ☐

   B It's impossible to play tennis in this weather. ☐

5 I think that wall will fall down unless they repair it.

   A They're going to repair the wall. ☐

   B Maybe they won't repair the wall. ☐

6 She wouldn't have so many pets if she didn't love animals.

   A She's got lots of pets. ☐

   B She hasn't got many pets. ☐

Grammar reference

13 Third conditional

Condition		Result
If	the bus **had come** on time,	we **would have got** here ten minutes ago.
	he**'d (had) driven** more carefully,	the accident **wouldn't have happened**.
	you **hadn't helped** me with this work,	I **wouldn't have known** how to do it.
	they**'d (had) been** here yesterday,	what **would** they **have done**?

● We use the third conditional when we are imagining a situation in the past that did not happen in reality. The action depends on a condition that is impossible because the past can't be changed.

*If we **had played** well, we **would have won** the match.* (But we didn't play well, so we didn't win.)

*If you**'d taken** an umbrella, you **wouldn't have got** wet.* (But you didn't take one, so you got wet.)

*If I **hadn't found** my keys, I **wouldn't have been** able to get inside.* (But I did find them, so I was able to get in.)

● In the *if* clause we use *had* + past participle. In the result clause, we use *would/wouldn't have* + past participle.

✱ We can use *might have*, *may have* or *could have* instead of *would have* if we are more uncertain about the result.

● We can change the order of the two clauses.

We would have won the match if we had played well.

You wouldn't have got wet if you'd taken an umbrella.

I wouldn't have been able to get inside if I hadn't found my keys.

14 *wish* and *if only*

	I **had** a better computer. this film **wasn't** so boring.
I wish **If only**	it **would stop** raining. they **wouldn't argue** all the time.
	we**'d (had) taken** some photos of the carnival. I **hadn't spent** all my money.

● We use *wish* and *if only* when we want something to be true, even though it is unlikely or impossible. *If only* is similar to *I wish*, but stronger.

● We use a past simple verb when we want a present situation to be different but can't change it.

*I wish I **lived** on a tropical island.* (But the reality is that I <u>don't</u> live there.)

*If only the tickets **didn't cost** so much!* (But they <u>do</u> cost a lot.)

● We use *would* + infinitive when we would like something/someone else to take action now or in the future. We have no power to make this happen.

*If only Joe **would lend** me his leather jacket!* (It's possible but unlikely that he will lend it to me.)

*I wish people **wouldn't park** their cars here.* (They could stop doing it, but they probably won't.)

● We use the past perfect when we regret an action or situation in the past.

*I wish I**'d brought** my sunglasses with me.* (But I <u>didn't</u> bring them and the past can't be changed.)

*If only you **hadn't wasted** so much time!* (But you <u>did</u> waste a lot of time.)

Grammar practice

13 Third conditional

a Match the two parts of the sentences.

1 If the river had flooded, ☐   **A** they'd put more ham on it.

2 I could have helped her if ☐   **B** she wouldn't have been late for work.

3 If she hadn't overslept, ☐   **C** she'd gone to the audition.

4 I would have enjoyed my pizza more if ☐   **D** she wouldn't have calmed down.

5 If I hadn't apologised to Helen, ☐   **E** she'd told me she was in trouble.

6 She might have got a part in the play if ☐   **F** it would have damaged hundreds of houses.

b Complete the sentences so that the meaning is the same. Use the third conditional.

1 When I called you, I didn't realise it was so late.

   I wouldn't ....

2 We looked at the map, so we didn't get lost.

   If we ....

3 He wanted to watch the quiz, but he fell asleep.

   He would ....

4 I went to the exhibition because you recommended it.

   If you ....

5 My white shirt wasn't clean, so I couldn't wear it.

   I could ....

6 We had to wait because the bus wasn't on time.

   If the bus ....

14 *wish* and *if only*

a Read the sentences with *wish* and *if only*. Is the following sentence *right* (✓) or *wrong* (✗)?

1 If only the letter would arrive!   I really want it to come soon. ☐

2 I wish you'd reminded me about Nick's birthday.   I'll forget if you don't remind me. ☐

3 I wish you liked this music.   I know you don't like it. ☐

4 If only I hadn't lost my watch!   I lost it and I'm sad about that. ☐

5 If only my feet didn't hurt!   I don't want to get sore feet. ☐

6 I wish Carla would hurry up.   I was annoyed because she was so slow! ☐

b Complete the sentences with the correct form of the verbs.

① ② ③

1 I wish I .... (know) the answers. If only I .... (study) for this test!

2 If only it .... (get) warmer! I wish I .... (not leave) my jacket at home.

3 If only Annie .... (not live) so far away! I wish she .... (ring) me.

Grammar reference

15

Permission: *can*, *let* and *be allowed to*

I	can can't 'm allowed to 'm not allowed to	go out at night.

My father	lets doesn't let	me	go out at night.

- *Can* and *be allowed to* mean 'to have permission from someone'. *Let* means 'to give permission'.

- *Can* is a modal verb. The past form is *could*. For the future we use *can* or *will be able to*.

  You **can borrow** my scarf.   Lisa was in detention, so she **couldn't go** home until 4pm.

  Can I **leave** the room, please?   I **won't be able to stay** out late tonight.

- *Be allowed* is the passive form of the verb *allow* (see Passives below). It is followed by *to* + infinitive.

  Are you **allowed to wear** jewellery at school?   They **weren't allowed to take** photos in the museum.

  I don't think we**'ll be allowed to bring** the dog into the restaurant.

- *Let* is an irregular verb: the past simple and past participle are also *let*. The form is *let* + object (a person) + infinitive.

  My sister **doesn't let me read** her diary.   Yesterday our teacher **let us leave** five minutes early.

  Will you **let me borrow** your phone?

16

Passives

Present simple passive							
It	's (is)	made written	of metal. in English.	It	isn't	made written	of metal. in English.
They	're (are)			They	aren't		
Is	it	made written	of metal? in English?	Yes, it **is**.		No, it **isn't**.	
Are	they			Yes, they **are**.		No, they **aren't**.	

- Most sentences are active. The subject does the action.

  Architects design buildings. (*Architects* is the subject and architects do the action of designing.)

- In a passive sentence the subject doesn't do the action. It is the 'receiver' of the action, which is done by something/someone else.

  Active

  Farmers grow a lot of coffee in Brazil.

  The police arrested two men yesterday.

  Passive

  *A lot of coffee **is grown** in Brazil.*

  *Two men **were arrested** yesterday.*

- We often use the passive when we don't know who/what does the action, or when it isn't important to identify them. If we want to say who/what does the action, we use *by*.

  *This poem was written **by** Shakespeare.   Buildings are often damaged **by** hurricanes.*

- We form passives with the verb *be* + past participle.

- Most tenses have a passive form. To make a present simple verb passive, we use the present simple form of *be*; for the past simple passive, we use the past simple form of *be*, and so on.

  Past simple: *When **were** these machines **invented**?*   Present continuous: *The bridge **is being repaired** now.*

  Present perfect: *Our house **has been burgled** three times.*   Past perfect: *By Monday morning, all the tickets **had been sold**.*

- We can also use modal verbs + *be* + past participle.

  *Their new album **will be released** next month.*   *This dish **can be served** with pasta or rice.*

  *Safety helmets **must be worn** on the building site.*   *Metal and plastic products **should be recycled**.*

Grammar practice

15 Permission: *can*, *let* and *be allowed to*

Rewrite the sentences so that the meaning is the same. Use the word in brackets.

1 Will you give me permission to use your phone?
  (can) ....

2 Julie's brother says she can't ride his skateboard.
  (let) ....

3 They don't let us leave school at lunch time.
  (allowed) ....

4 He has his parents' permission to drive the car.
  (let) ....

5 In most countries they didn't let women vote a hundred years ago.
  (couldn't) ....

6 I didn't have permission to go to the disco.
  (wasn't) ....

16 Passives

a Choose the correct answer: A, B or C.

1 This bag .... made in China but I bought it
  in London.
  A is   **B** was   **C** has

2 The builders .... a lot of work on the roof.
  A have done   **B** are done   **C** have been done

3 The film will .... in a few weeks' time.
  A release   **B** released   **C** be released

4 In warm weather butter should .... in the fridge.
  A keep   **B** kept   **C** be kept

5 The plane .... off until 11:45.
  A didn't take **B** isn't taken **C** wasn't taken

6 Why .... the timetable been changed?
  A was   **B** has   **C** will

c Rewrite the sentences in the passive.

1 Someone left a bag in the restaurant.
  ....

2 People don't use this water for drinking.
  ....

3 The flood has damaged several buildings.
  ....

4 Will they finish the new sports centre soon?
  ....

5 You must not eat food in the classrooms.
  ....

b One word is wrong in each line of this text. ~~Cross out~~ the wrong word and write the correct one.

These are some of the entries that have be accepted for	1 ....
the Young Painters competition. They were all paint by	2 ....
local artists under the age of 18 and they can been seen at	3 ....
the Blake Gallery. A prize of £1,000 has given every year	4 ....
for the best painting. The winner will be chose by three	5 ....
judges and the result has be announced next Saturday.	6 ....

Grammar reference

17 Modal verbs of deduction

Present

Not sure					
Positive			**Negative**		
It They	**might** **may** **could**	**be** French.	It They	**might not** **may not**	**be** French.
Sure					
Positive			**Negative**		
You She	**must**	**be** French.	You She	**can't**	**be** French.

- We use modal verbs to make guesses about a present situation.

- The form is modal + infinitive and this form is the same for all subjects.

- We use *might*, *may* or *could* when we think something is possibly true but we aren't sure. For the negative we use *might not* or *may not* (but **not** ~~couldn't~~).

  *A: What is it? B: I don't know. It **might / may / could be** a type of insect.*
  *I think this is her best record, but you **might/may not agree** with me.*

- We use *must* if we are sure something is true and *can't* (**not** ~~mustn't~~) if we are sure something is not true.

  *They come from Chile, so they **must speak** Spanish.*
  *It's just an ordinary plastic watch. It **can't be** expensive.*

- *Might*, *may*, *could* and *must* + infinitive can refer to the future as well as the present.

  *I haven't decided on a present for Mum yet. I **might buy** her a scarf.*
  *We're not sure when she'll arrive. She **may not be** here in time for dinner.*
  *Carlos has been asleep for nine hours! He **must wake** up soon.*

Past

Not sure					
Positive			**Negative**		
I He	**might** **may** **could**	**have seen** this film.	I He	**might not** **may not**	**have seen** this film.
Sure					
Positive			**Negative**		
You They	**must**	**have seen** this film.	You They	**can't**	**have seen** this film.

- We use the same modal verbs + *have* + past participle to make guesses about a past situation or action.

- We use *might have*, *may have* or *could have* when we think something possibly happened in the past but we aren't sure.

  *I don't know where they went. They **might / may / could have gone** to the bookshop.*
  *I sent the postcard a few days ago, but she **might/may not have received** it yet.*

- We use *must have* if we are sure something happened. We use *can't have* if we are sure something didn't happen.

  *Pete isn't working at the garage now. He **must have found** a new job.*
  *I'm sure you had your sunglasses when you came in. You **can't have lost** them.*

Grammar practice

17 Modal verbs of deduction

a Choose the correct answer: A, B or C.

1 Alice hasn't eaten anything all day, so I'm sure she .... be hungry now.

   A must   **B** could   **C** can't

2 Martin .... be at home. He sometimes goes to the gym on Thursdays.

   A must   **B** can't   **C** might not

3 You .... like this song but I'm not very keen on it.

   A may   **B** may not   **C** might not

4 The bird is tiny. It .... weigh more than a few grams.

   A must   **B** mustn't   **C** can't

5 Hang on a minute, I'll just check my phone. I .... have a message from Roberto.

   A can   **B** could   **C** must

6 I don't think you should touch those cables. They .... be safe.

   A may   **B** may not   **C** might

b Tick (✓) the sentence if it is correct. If there is a mistake, ~~cross out~~ the wrong word(s) and write the correct word(s). Sometimes there is more than one possible answer.

1 I told Dave about the audition, but he could have forgot. ....

2 It was getting dark, so they may not of seen us. ....

3 Someone must have had an accident – there's broken glass everywhere. ....

4 Danny left half an hour ago, but he might not have got home yet. ....

5 Emma must have gone to the supermarket, but I'm not sure. ....

6 They mustn't have had lunch in the café yesterday because it was closed. ....

c Complete the dialogues. Use the verbs with modals. Sometimes there is more than one possible answer.

Mike: I like those shoes, but they ¹........................... (be) expensive. Everything costs a lot in this shop.

Chris: Why don't you check out the internet? They ²........................... .... (be) cheaper online.

Mike: Yeah, maybe.

Chris: Tim's got a pair like those and he ³........................... (not pay) a huge amount for them. He never has much money and he hates spending a lot on clothes and shoes.

Lisa: I saw Caroline at the market yesterday.

Petra: No, it ⁴........................... (not be) Caroline. She's staying with her aunt in Scotland. You ⁵........................... .... (see) someone who looked like her.

Lisa: How can you be sure? She ⁶........................... (decide) to come home early.

Petra: No, she sent me a text this morning from Edinburgh, so she ⁷........................... still .... (be) there.

Grammar reference

18 Quantifiers

enough and *too*

● We use *enough* to mean 'the amount/number that is needed'.

*He couldn't go skiing – there wasn't **enough snow**.   Have we got **enough sandwiches** for everyone?*

● We use *too much* + uncountable noun and *too many* + plural noun to mean 'more than what is wanted or acceptable'.

*Yuk! There's **too much sugar** in this coffee.   They'd invited **too many people**. No one could move!*

● We also use *enough* and *too* with adjectives. *Enough* goes after the adjective but *too* goes before it.

*I can't hear the music properly. It isn't **loud enough**.   You can't carry that on your own. It's **too heavy**.*

a few, *fewer* and *less*

● We use *a few* + plural noun to describe a small number.

*We spent **a few days** in Cairo.   I'm going to ask **a few friends** to come to dinner.*

● *Fewer* and *less* are comparative words. We use *fewer* + plural noun to mean 'a smaller number'. We use *less* + uncountable noun to mean 'a smaller amount'.

*There were **fewer cars** on the road 50 years ago.   Take the train. It takes **less time** than the bus.*

● We can also use *less* + adjective.

*Fish are **less intelligent** than dolphins.   This type of phone is **less expensive** than it used to be.*

19 Non-defining relative clauses

Main clause	Relative clause	
One of my best friends is Nikos,	**who**	comes from Greece.
		you met the other day.
	whose	father owns a Greek restaurant.
I bought some new shoes,	**which**	will look good with my black jeans.
		I wore for the first time yesterday.
We often go to the Red Rose Café,	**where**	you can always get a good cheap meal.

● A relative clause refers to someone or something earlier in the sentence.

● A defining relative clause gives essential information. A non-defining relative clause is not essential but adds extra information. It is separated from the rest of the sentence by commas.

Defining: *People **who love animals** will enjoy this programme.*

Non-defining: *Angela, **who loves animals**, was watching a programme about bears.*

> ✱ In defining relative clauses we can use *that* instead of *who* or *which*. In non-defining relative clauses we do not use *that*.

● We use *who* for people.

*I got some help from <u>my sister</u>, **who** is very good at Maths.*

● We use *whose* for people when we want to talk about something that belongs to them. *Whose* is a possessive form which we use instead of *his*, *her* or *their*. It is always followed by a noun.

*<u>Mr Jones</u>, **whose** [house] is opposite ours, is a dentist.   That's <u>Ellie</u>, **whose** [mother] teaches at our school.*

● We use *which* for things.

*We had some <u>grapes</u>, **which** were delicious.   The <u>volcano</u>, **which** last erupted in 1980, is still active.*

● We use *where* for places. It means 'in which', 'at which' or 'to which' and is followed by a noun or pronoun.

*This <u>beach</u>, **where** [lots of surfers] go, is often too crowded.   He went to the <u>gym</u>, **where** [he] met Sam.*

Grammar practice

18 Quantifiers

a Complete the sentences with *too*, *too much*, *too many* or *enough*.

1 Don't eat .... chocolate biscuits. They aren't good for you.
2 We haven't got .... eggs to make a cake.
3 I won't be able to watch TV tonight. I've got .... homework.
4 Those folders won't fit in your bag. They're .... big.
5 Do you think Ronaldo will be fit .... to play in next Saturday's match?
6 It's not a big problem. He's giving it .... importance.

b Rewrite the sentences so that the meaning is the same. Use the word in brackets.

1 We've bought more milk than we need. (too) ....
2 I need some more batteries. (enough) ....
3 Our old dishwasher made more noise than our new one. (less) ....
4 I'll be ready in two or three minutes. (few) ....
5 These jeans aren't big enough for me. (small) ....
6 More people used to study Latin in the past. (now) ....

19 Non-defining relative clauses

a Match the two parts of the sentences.

1 Dad's motorbike, ..., is a Harley-Davidson. ☐
2 The policeman, ..., gave us directions to the station. ☐
3 That's the Old Trafford stadium, ... ☐
4 My favourite shop is New Fashions, ... ☐
5 I'm going to give this card to Patrick, ... ☐
6 Those two people, ..., live in the flat above ours. ☐

A where Manchester United play
B who we haven't met
C whose birthday is on Thursday
D which he bought in 1994
E who was very helpful
F which sells interesting clothes

b Complete each sentence with a relative clause. Use words from each box and add commas.

who   which   whose
~~where~~   where

owns the music shop behind her   name is Mr Foster
~~Hive~~   people are having coffee   is that building on the corner

1 This picture shows the town of Lilydale,
   ..where I live.. .
2 My friend Steve is talking to the woman with long hair
   ....
3 The man on the right ....
   .... is our next-door neighbour.
4 Mrs Foster is coming out of the post office ....
   ....
5 The Paragon Café ....
   .... was built in the 1930s.

Grammar reference

20 · *as if, as though* and *like*

- We use *as if*, *as though* and *like* to describe how a situation seems to be. They often follow verbs of sensation (*look*, *feel*, *sound*, *taste*) and the verb *seem*.

- *As if* and *as though* are followed by a full clause, with a subject + a verb.
  *It seems **as if / as though** the sun is moving, but really it's the Earth.*
  *David was sitting there with his eyes closed. He looked **as if / as though** he was sleeping.*

- *Like* can also be followed by a clause, but this use is informal.
  *Hey Fiona, what's wrong? You look **like** you've seen a ghost!*

- *Like* normally means 'similar to' and is followed by a noun or an *-ing* word used as a noun.
  *Jack looks **like** his father. They've got the same eyes and mouth.*
  *I'm so uncomfortable on this chair! It's **like** sitting on a rock.*

21 · *a/an, the* or no article

- *A/an* means 'one of many' and it always goes with a singular countable noun. We are referring to a person/thing that is not identified specifically. This may be a general type of person/thing.
  *Have you ever been in **a** helicopter?*   *I think I'll have **an apple**.*
  *We've got **a** new **teacher** for Science.*   *This is **a machine** for making bread.*
  *My sister wants to be **an architect**.*

- *The* means 'the particular one(s)'. We are referring to a specific person, thing or group.
  *Sandro is wearing **the shirt** <u>that I gave him</u>. (I'm identifying the particular shirt that I mean.)*
  *I love **the music** <u>on this album</u>.*
  ***The students** <u>in Helen's class</u> are organising a concert.*
  ***The sun** was shining brightly. (We have only one sun, so this is a specific thing.)*
  *Let's go to **the gym** later. (The gym we always go to – you know the one I mean.)*

- We use *a/an* for someone/something that we are mentioning for the first time. When this person/thing is mentioned again, we use *the*.
  *When I looked out the window, I noticed **a** black car outside. There were two people in **the** car.*

- We use no article with uncountable and plural nouns when we are referring to something or things/people in general.
  ***Cheese** is made from **milk**.*   (But ***The cheese** <u>that is made in this area</u> is called Roquefort.)
  ***Information** can be found on the internet.*
  ***Women** used to wear long **dresses**.*
  *She doesn't like speaking to **journalists**.*

- We use no article for these expressions with places:

go home	at home	go to bed	in bed
go to school	at school	go to prison	in prison
go to university	at university	go to hospital	in hospital
go to work	at work		

- There is no article with names of languages. There is also usually no article with names of places. The exception is when the place name is plural or has an adjective which is not a direction (*North*, *South*, etc.).
  *People speak **Spanish** in **Argentina**.*   *He comes from **South Africa**.*
  *(But **the** Philippines, **the** United States, **the** Czech Republic)*

Grammar practice

20 *as if, as though* and *like*

Complete the sentences. Use *as if, as though* or *like* and the words in the box.

> you're on a ship   it might snow soon   a photograph   walking into a freezer
> the film is excellent   the one that James bought

1 All the reviews are very positive. It sounds ....
2 That painting is so realistic! It's ....
3 From the front window you look out over the sea. It feels ....
4 I'd like to find a jacket ....
5 The cold air really hits you when you go outside. It's ....
6 Look at those clouds. It looks ....

21 *a/an, the* or no article

a Circle the correct words.

1 That's *a / the* shop where Pete works on Saturdays.
2 My aunt lives in *a / the* town in *Portugal / the Portugal*.
3 I like wearing *jeans / the jeans* and *T-shirts / the T-shirts*.
4 We're doing *experiment / an experiment* with *electricity / an electricity*.
5 Everest is *a / the* highest mountain in *world / the world*.
6 Emily wants to do *a / the* Science course when she goes to *university / the university*.

b Complete the text with *a, an, the* or leave the space blank where no article is needed.

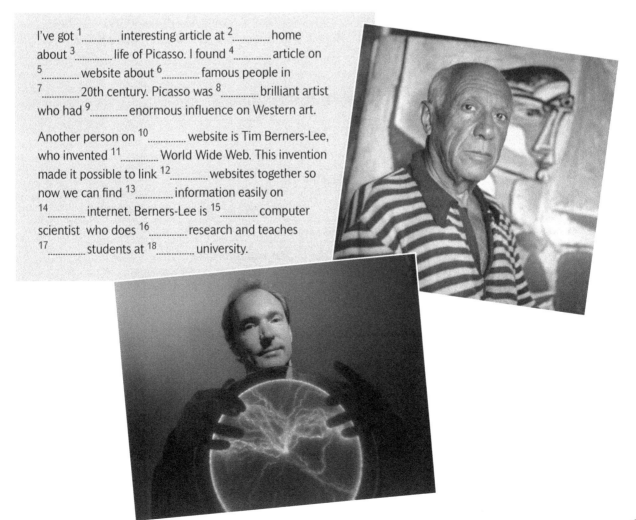

I've got [1] .... interesting article at [2] .... home
about [3] .... life of Picasso. I found [4] .... article on
[5] .... website about [6] .... famous people in
[7] .... 20th century. Picasso was [8] .... brilliant artist
who had [9] .... enormous influence on Western art.

Another person on [10] .... website is Tim Berners-Lee,
who invented [11] .... World Wide Web. This invention
made it possible to link [12] .... websites together so
now we can find [13] .... information easily on
[14] .... internet. Berners-Lee is [15] .... computer
scientist who does [16] .... research and teaches
[17] .... students at [18] .... university.

Grammar reference

22 : Reported statements

Direct speech	Reported speech
present simple Amir: 'I **want** a sandwich.'	past simple Amir said (that) he **wanted** a sandwich.
present continuous Sofia: 'The TV **isn't working**.'	past continuous Sofia said (that) the TV **wasn't working**.
present perfect Daniel: 'The plane **hasn't landed**.'	past perfect Daniel said (that) the plane **hadn't landed**.
past simple Petra: 'I **saw** Nick at the cinema.'	past perfect Petra said (that) she **had seen** Nick at the cinema.
will Oliver: 'I**'ll** help with the cooking.'	*would* Oliver said (that) he **would** help with the cooking.
can Yasmin: 'They **can't** sing very well.'	*could* Yasmin said (that) they **couldn't** sing very well.

- When we report what someone said, the tense usually changes. The verb usually moves 'one step back' into the past.

- Pronouns and possessive adjectives may need to change in the reported statement.

  Enzo: '**My** friends are waiting for **me**.' Enzo said that **his** friends were waiting for **him**.
  Mia: '**We** met **your** cousin in the park.' Mia told me **they** had met **my** cousin in the park.

- Other words indicating time and place may also need to change.

  'We'll be at home **this evening / today**.' He told me they would be at home **that evening/day**.
  'I'm leaving **tomorrow / next week**.' She said she was leaving **the next day / the following week**.
  'I lost my keys **yesterday / last Sunday**.' Tom said he had lost his keys **the previous day / Sunday**.
  'I've never been **here** before.' Antonia told us that she had never been **there** before.

23 : Reported questions, commands and requests

Question		Reported question
'Where **are** they **going**?' 'Who **did** you **speak** to?' '**Do** you **like** playing tennis?' '**Will** Sara **be** at the party?'	She **asked** me	where they **were going**. who I **had spoken** to. **if/whether** I **liked** playing tennis. **if/whether** Sara **would be** at the party.
Command		**Reported command**
'**Stop** shouting!' '**Don't leave** your bike outside.'	He **told** me	**to stop** shouting. **not to leave** my bike outside.
Request		**Reported request**
'**Please help** me.' '**Can/Could you help** me, please?'	He **asked** us	**to help** him.

- When we report a question that someone asked, we express their question in the form of a statement. The reporting verb is usually *ask*. The rules for tenses, pronouns, etc. are the same as for reported statements.

- For an information question, we repeat the question word. For a *yes/no* question, we use *if* or *whether*.

- When we report a command, the form is *tell* someone *(not) to* + infinitive.

- When we report a request, the form is *ask* someone *to* + infinitive.

> ✱ *Tell* and *ask* are followed by a noun or pronoun object (= the person who was told/asked).
>
> *He told **me** to stop.*
> *He asked **us** to help.*

Grammar practice

22 Reported statements

a There is a mistake in each reported statement. ~~Cross out~~ the wrong word(s) and write the correct word(s).

1 'I don't really want to play basketball.'
Simon said I didn't really want to play basketball.   ....

2 'You'll need a good pair of walking boots.'
Katherine told me I'll need a good pair of walking boots.   ....

3 'We're going on a school trip to the museum.'
Omar said they went on a school trip to the museum.   ....

4 'I can't remember if I've been here before.'
Adam said he can't remember if he'd been there before.   ....

5 'I think someone has stolen my purse.'
Manuela said she thought someone stole her purse.   ....

b Rewrite the <u>underlined</u> words as reported speech.

Matt: ¹<u>I'm trying to write my poetry essay</u>, but ²<u>it's difficult</u>. Will you look at it with me?

Hana: OK, but not right now. ³<u>I promised to meet Jess this afternoon</u> and ⁴<u>I'm already late</u>.

Matt: ⁵<u>I really need some help</u>, Hana. ⁶<u>I can't understand the poem</u> and ⁷<u>I've already spent an hour on it</u>.

Hana: Don't worry. ⁸<u>I'll help you</u> when ⁹<u>I get home</u>.

Matt said ¹.., but ².. .

Hana said ³.. and ⁴.. .

Matt told Hana that ⁵.. .

He said ⁶.. and ⁷.. .

Hana said ⁸.. when ⁹.. .

23 Reported questions, commands and requests

a Circle the correct answer: A, B or C.

1	I .... my friend Kim to lend me £5.	A said	B asked	C had
2	Sophie asked us .... we were going to the beach.	A where	B what	C whether
3	The teacher asked me what .... doing.	A I'm	B I was	C was I
4	My parents told me .... home before midnight.	A come	B I come	C to come
5	Isabel asked us if we .... her brother.	A saw	B 've seen	C had seen
6	Dad asked me where .... been.	A I had	B had I	C have I

b Complete the sentences. Use reported speech with *asked* or *told*.

1 'Where does your brother work?'   She .... me ....

2 'Leave your bags here.'   The teacher .... us ....

3 'Could you open the door, please?'   A woman .... me ....

4 'Did you get my email?'   He .... Anna ....

5 'When will the train get here?'   She .... us ....

6 'Put your rubbish in the bin.'   Mr Scott .... them ....

Grammar reference

24: Subject and object questions

Object questions	Subject questions
Who **do you live** with?	Who **lives** in that house?
What **did Matt do**?	What **happened** to Matt?
Which band **are they watching**?	Which band **is playing** tonight?
How many people **can you see**?	How many people **can see** us?

Object questions

- Object questions are the most common type of information question. They can start with any question word.

- Object questions have a noun or pronoun subject.

  *Where **did she go**?* (*she* is the subject)

  *What **do they have** for breakfast?* (*they* is the subject)

  *Which team **is your father supporting**?* (*your father* is the subject)

  *Why **should people recycle** their rubbish?* (*people* is the subject)

- Object questions always contain an auxiliary verb (a form of *be*, *do* or *have*) or a modal verb (*can*, *will*, *should*, etc.).

- The form is question word + auxiliary/modal + subject + main verb form.

Subject questions

- A subject question can only start with *Who*, *Whose*, *What*, *Which* or *How much/many*.

- In subject questions the subject is the question word.

  *Who **has taken** my keys?* (*Who* is the subject)

  *What **is making** that noise?* (*What* is the subject)

  *How many people **can go** on the boat trip?* (*How many people* is the subject)

- The verb is in the form of a statement. This means that in the present and past simple there is no auxiliary verb.

  *What **makes** this machine work?* (**not** What ~~does make~~)

  *Who **won** the prize?* (**not** Who ~~did win~~)

- The form is question word + verb.

25: *would rather* and *would prefer*

- We use *would rather* and *would prefer* to express a particular preference for something to happen now or in the future.

  *I**'d prefer to read** than play video games tonight.*

  *We**'d rather go** to Venice than Rome for our next holiday.*

  *I've got a cold, so I**'d rather not go** out tonight.*

  ***Would** you **prefer to have** cake or biscuits with your coffee?*

  *What **would** you **rather watch** now – the news or the football?*

> ✱ Note the difference between *I'd prefer* and *I prefer*. *Prefer …ing* or *prefer to* expresses a general preference that is always true.
>
> *I **prefer skiing** to snowboarding.*
>
> *My sister **prefers to** get up early.*

- The forms are *would rather* + infinitive and *would prefer* + *to* + infinitive.

- We can also use *would rather* + person + past simple to say what we would like someone else to do.

  *I**'d rather** you **didn't bring** the dog inside, if you don't mind.*

  *I want to do an Art course, but my parents **would rather** I **studied** Medicine.*

Grammar practice

24 Subject and object questions

a Which question is *right* (✓) and which is *wrong* (✗)?

1 **A** What you did on Friday night? ☐
  B What did you do on Friday night? ☐

2 **A** How much money he needs? ☐
  B How much money does he need? ☐

3 **A** What type of music you like? ☐
  B What type of music do you like? · ☐

4 **A** Who left these books here? ☐
  B Who did they leave these books here? ☐

5 **A** Which student came top in the exam? ☐
  B Which student did come top in the exam? ☐

6 **A** Who wants to invite to the party? ☐
  B Who do they want to invite to the party? ☐

b Complete the questions.

I want to know:

1 the number of people who went to the concert. How many ....?
2 what George wants for his birthday. What ....?
3 the name of the person who wrote *Hamlet*. Who ....?
4 the name of the record label that produced this album. Which ....?
5 the amount of time Nadia spent at the gym. How much ....?
6 the names of the people who teach Art at your school. Who ....?

c Write the subject or object questions.

1 Who / you / usually / have / lunch with?

....

2 What / happen / yesterday morning?

....

3 How many sandwiches / you / want?

....

4 Which songs / they / download / last night?

....

5 Who / give / you / those earrings?

....

6 What / she / like / doing in her free time?

....

25 *would rather* and *would prefer*

Complete the dialogues.

1 **A:** What shall we have with the meal – vegetables or salad?
  B: I .... (prefer / have) salad.

2 **A:** Will they be watching the tennis on TV tonight?
  B: No, I think they .... (rather / watch) a movie.

3 **A:** .... (you / prefer / go) to the market or to the shopping centre?
  B: Let's go to the market.

4 **A:** Do you want to talk to Liam?
  B: No, I .... (rather / you / speak) to him.

5 **A:** Will Tara try to get a job this summer?
  B: Probably not. I think she .... (prefer / not work) during the holidays.

6 **A:** We could ask Jamie to bring his drums on Saturday.
  B: Actually, I .... (rather / he / not bring) them. There won't be enough room for them!

Irregular verbs

Verb	Past simple	Past participle	Verb	Past simple	Past participle
be	was/were	been	let	let	let
beat	beat	beaten	lose	lost	lost
become	became	become	make	made	made
begin	began	begun	mean	meant	meant
blow	blew	blown	meet	met	met
break	broke	broken	oversleep	overslept	overslept
bring	brought	brought	pay	paid	paid
build	built	built	put	put	put
burn	burned/burnt	burned/burnt	read	read	read
buy	bought	bought	ride	rode	ridden
can	could	been able	ring	rang	rung
catch	caught	caught	rise	rose	risen
choose	chose	chosen	run	ran	run
come	came	come	say	said	said
cost	cost	cost	see	saw	seen
cut	cut	cut	sell	sold	sold
do	did	done	send	sent	sent
draw	drew	drawn	set	set	set
drink	drank	drunk	shake	shook	shaken
drive	drove	driven	shoot	shot	shot
eat	ate	eaten	show	showed	shown
fall	fell	fallen	shut	shut	shut
feel	felt	felt	sing	sang	sung
fight	fought	fought	sit	sat	sat
find	found	found	speak	spoke	spoken
fly	flew	flown	spell	spelled/spelt	spelled/spelt
forget	forgot	forgotten	spend	spent	spent
get	got	got	spin	span/spun	spun
give	gave	given	stand	stood	stood
go	went	gone/been	steal	stole	stolen
grow	grew	grown	swim	swam	swum
have	had	had	swing	swung	swung
hear	heard	heard	take	took	taken
hide	hid	hidden	teach	taught	taught
hit	hit	hit	tell	told	told
hold	held	held	think	thought	thought
hurt	hurt	hurt	throw	threw	thrown
keep	kept	kept	understand	understood	understood
know	knew	known	wake	woke	woken
learn	learned/learnt	learned/learnt	wear	wore	worn
leave	left	left	win	won	won
lend	lent	lent	write	wrote	written

Phonemic chart

Consonant sounds

/b/
bird

/tʃ/
cheese

/d/
door

/f/
fish

/g/
girl

/h/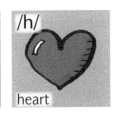
heart

/dʒ/
jam

/k/
key

/l/
leaf

/m/
monkey

/n/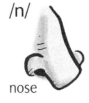
nose

/ŋ/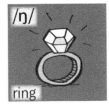
ring

/p/
pen

/r/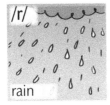
rain

/s/
sofa

/ʃ/
shoe

/ʒ/
television

/t/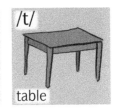
table

/ð/
feather

/θ/
think

/v/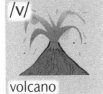
volcano

/w/
window

/j/
yoga

/z/
zoo

Vowel sounds

/æ/
apple

/e/
head

/ɪ/
insect

/ɒ/
hot

/ʌ/
umbrella

/ʊ/
book

/ɑː/
arm

/ɜː/
earth

/iː/
sheep

/ɔː/
ball

/uː/
moon

/eə/
chair

/ɪə/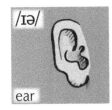
ear

/aɪ/
eye

/eɪ/
paper

/ɔɪ/
boy

/əʊ/
phone

/aʊ/
owl

/ə/
computer

Go to the Interactive website to download the workbook audio.

www.cambridge.org/interactive